BELLY LAUGHS FOR ALL!

Adult Version
Volume 5

ROBERTA CAVA

Copyright © 2016 by Roberta Cava

All rights reserved. No part of this work covered by the copyrights hereon may be reproduced or used in any form or by any means - graphic, electronic or mechanical, including photocopying, recording, taping or information storage and retrieval systems - without the prior written permission of the publisher.

Belly Laughs for All!
Adult Version
Volume 5
Roberta Cava

Published by Cava Consulting

info@dealingwithdifficultpeople.info

Discover other titles by Roberta Cava at
www.dealingwithdifficultpeople.info

National Library of Australia
Cataloguing-in-publication data:

ISBN 978-0-9944365-2-8

BOOKS BY ROBERTA CAVA

Non-Fiction

Dealing with Difficult People
(22 publishers - in 16 languages)
Dealing with Difficult Situations – at Work and at Home
Dealing with Difficult Spouses and Children
Dealing with Difficult Relatives and In-Laws
Dealing with Domestic Violence and Child Abuse
Dealing with School Bullying
Dealing with Workplace Bullying
Retirement Village Bullies
New: Keeping our children safe
What am I going to do with the rest of my life?
Before tying the knot – Questions couples Must ask each other
Before they marry!
How Women can advance in business
Survival Skills for Supervisors and Managers
Human Resources at its Best!
Human Resources Policies and Procedures
Employee Handbooks
Easy Come – Hard to go – The Art of Hiring, Disciplining and Firing Employees
Time and Stress – Today's silent killers
Take Command of your Future – Make things Happen
Belly Laughs for All! – Volumes 1 to 5
Wisdom of the World

Fiction

That Something Special
Something Missing
Trilogy: Life Gets Complicated
Life Goes On
Life Gets Better

BELLY LAUGHS FOR ALL!

Volume 5

Table of Contents

Introduction	1
Chapter 1 – Couples	5
Chapter 2 – Males	21
Chapter 3 – Females	29
Chapter 4 – Lawyers	33
Chapter 5 – Doctors	37
Chapter 6 – Police	47
Chapter 7 – Travel	53
Chapter 8 – Children	61
Chapter 9 – Seniors	75
Chapter 10 – Blondes	87
Chapter 11 – Religions	93
Chapter 12 – At Work	107
Chapter 13 – Is that right?	119
Chapter 14 – Miscellaneous	135
Chapter 15 – History	149
Chapter 16 – Bar	175
Chapter 17 – High Technology	181
Chapter 18 – Rules for Living	185
Chapter 19 – On the serious side	195
Conclusion	205

INTRODUCTION

Most of my books relate to how to deal with difficult people and situations. I had been feeling very depressed after writing my last three books - which focused around bullying - at home, at school and at work. This was a lovely change from that disturbing and depressing research.

I had collected jokes for years and enjoyed reading them whenever I felt down-in-the-dumps. This is what stimulated me to write books on humour. It was soon evident that I had too many jokes for just one volume, hence I wrote Volumes 1, 2, 3, 4 and this is Volume 5. They discuss humour in different areas, so there's no repetition. I also realised that the books were meant for adult audiences and ***are not suitable for children***.

I hope you enjoy this volume enough to want to obtain the other four volumes.

Belly Laughs for All – Volume 5

CHAPTER 1

COUPLES

Lost wife:

Two guys, one old, one young, are pushing their carts around Wal-Mart when they collide.

The old guy says to the young guy, 'Sorry about that. I'm looking for my wife, and I guess I wasn't paying attention to where I was going.'

The young guy says, 'That's okay, it's a coincidence. I'm looking for my wife, too... I can't find her and I'm getting a little desperate.'

The old guy says, 'Well, maybe I can help you find her... what does she look like?'

The young guy says, 'Well, she's 27 years old, tall, with red hair, blue eyes, is buxom...wearing no bra, long legs, and is wearing short shorts. What does your wife look like?'

To which the old guy replies, 'Doesn't matter, - let's look for yours.'

The final word

My wife and I had words, but I didn't get to use mine.

God made man before woman so as to give him time to think of an answer for her first question.

Frozen window:

Wife texts husband on a cold winter morning: 'Windows frozen, won't open.'

Husband texts back: 'Gently pour some lukewarm water over it and gently tap edges with hammer.'

Wife texts back five minutes later: 'Computer really messed up now.'

This 'N That:

- A bookseller conducting a market survey asked a woman: 'Which book has helped you most in your life?' The woman replied – 'My husband's cheque book!'
- A prospective husband in a book store 'Do you have a book called, 'Husband – the Master of the House?'
  Sales Girl: 'Sir, fiction and comics are on the first floor!'
- Portly man to wife: 'I'm on an exercise program. I have to walk three miles a day.'
  'That's great. This time next week you'll be twenty-one miles away.'
- Man to wife: 'Sure I'd love a second honeymoon – who with?'
- Nobody teaches volcanoes to erupt, tsunamis to devastate, hurricanes to swirl around and no one teaches a man how to choose a wife. Natural disasters just happen.
- Someone asked an old man: 'Even after 70 years, you still call your wife – Darling, Honey, Luv. What's the secret?'
  Old man: 'I forgot her name and I'm scared to ask her.'
- A man in Hell asked the Devil: 'Can I make a call to my wife?'
  After making the call he asked how much he had to pay.
  Devil: 'Nothing. Hell to hell is Free.'
- Wife: 'I wish I was a newspaper. So I'd be in your hands all day.'
  Husband: 'I too wish that you were a newspaper. So I could have a new one every day!'
- Woman buys a new Sim Card, puts it in her phone and decides to surprise her husband who is seated on the couch in the living room. She goes to the kitchen, calls her husband with the new number: 'Hello darling.'
  The husband responds in a low tone: 'Let me call you back later Sweetie, my wife is in the kitchen.'

- The difference between divorce and legal separation is that legal separation gives a husband time to hide his money.
- Make love, not war. Hell, do both and get married.
- Low battery: A man saved his girlfriend's phone number on his mobile as 'Low Battery.' Whenever she calls him in his absence, his wife takes the phone and plugs it into the charger. Give that man a medal.
- A married man can forget his mistakes. There's no use two people remembering the same thing!
- A woman marries a man expecting that he will change, but he doesn't. A man marries a woman expecting that she won't change – but she does.
- A woman has the last word in any argument. Anything a man says after that is the beginning of a new argument.
- A 'perfect marriage' is just two imperfect people who refuse to give up on each other.
- Judging by the frying pan that just flew by my head, I did something wrong. I can't wait to find out what it was.
- A husband is someone who, after taking the rubbish out, gives the impression he's just cleaned the whole house.
- Bigamy is having one wife too many. Monogamy is the same.
- Fred and Harry were walking down the street. Fred asks Harry how his wife is. Harry replies, 'She's struggling with the grog. She used to be able to carry a slab, now she has trouble with a six-pack.'
- Husband to wife: 'Today is a fine day. The next day he says: 'Today is a fine day.' Again the next day, he says same thing. Finally, after a week, the wife can't take it and asks her husband: 'Since last week, you've been saying "Today is a fine day'. I'm fed up. What's the matter?'

Husband: 'Last week when we had an argument, you said, 'I will leave you one fine day.' I was just trying to remind you.'

- Once upon a time, a guy asked a beautiful girl, 'Will you marry me?'
The girl said, 'No!' and the guy lived happily ever after and rode motorcycles and went fishing and hunting and played golf a lot and drank beer and scotch and had tons of money in the bank and left the toilet seat up and farted whenever he wanted. The end.

- 'I'll never forget how happy I was when I saw my missus walking down the aisle towards me. My heart was beating fast and the excitement was unbearable. It seemed to take an age, but eventually, there she was, standing beside me. I gave her a loving smile and said, 'Get that trolley over there, Love. They're offering three cartons of beer for the price of two!'

- After a quarrel, a wife said to her husband, 'You know, I was a fool when I married you.'
And the husband replied, 'Yes dear, but I was in love and didn't notice.'

- I got home and found the missus had left a post-it-note on the fridge saying, 'It's no good, it's not working. I'm staying at mom's for a while.'
I opened the fridge, the light came on, the beer was well chilled. Buggered if I know she was on about?'

- Experts tell us the best way to make a perfect cup of tea is to agitate the bag. So, every morning I shout, 'Two sugars, fat arse!'

- A married couple were having a terrible fight. The wife was screaming at the husband, 'Leave! Get out of this house!'
As her hubby was walking out the door she continued to yell, 'I hope you die a slow and painful death!'
Without missing a beat, the man stopped, turned around and replied, 'So now you want me to stay?'

- A couple had their first baby. After a week or so, the mother thought she could use a break and went shopping – leaving the little baby with the proud father.
  It was only a short while before the baby started to cry. The perplexed father tried all the tricks he remembered his wife doing, but to no avail. Finally after a half-hour and in desperation, he went to the doctor.
  After checking all of the regular things, the doctor discovered it was just a dirty nappy.
  'I don't understand,' the perplexed father said, 'I knew it was dirty, but the diaper package said specifically that it was good up to 5 kilograms.
- I was sent to prison and I said to me cell mate, 'I won't be in here long.'
  He replied, 'Well the judge did give you six ears.'
  'Yeah I know, but I think my wife will break me out. She's never let me finish a sentence before.'
- Neighbour to mother of four young children, 'How do you divide your love among four children?'
  'I don't divide it. I multiply it.'
- A descendant of Eric the Red, named Rudolf The Red, was arguing with his wife about the weather. His wife thought it was going to be a nice day, and he thought it was going to rain. Finally, she asked him, how he could be so sure. He smiled at her and calmly said, 'Because Rudolf The Red knows rain, dear.' (groan).
- It was the first night of the newlyweds in their bridal suite and the young husband was staring out the window very intently into the starry night while his young bride was sitting patiently in bed waiting.
  'Aren't you coming to bed darling?' she asked.
  'Not on your life!' he replied. 'My mom said this would be the most wonderful night of my life and I'm not going to miss it for anything!'
- After twenty-five years together, a couple went to marriage counselling. The counsellor asked what the problem was, and immediately the wife began a tirade

of complaints. He doesn't listen to me; he doesn't help around the house and so on.

After what seemed like an eternity the counsellor got up, walked around the desk, asked the wife to stand and then kissed her long and passionately as her husband watched.

The woman, now speechless, quietly sat down, dazed.

The counsellor turned to the husband and said, 'This is what your wife needs at least three times a week. Can you do this?'

The husband replied, 'Well I can drop her off here on Mondays and Wednesdays, but on Fridays I go fishing.'

- A couple about to be married become nervous as the big day approaches. The groom-to-be goes to his father for advice.

'Dad,' he says, 'I'm deeply concerned about the success of my marriage. You see, I have very smelly feet and I'm afraid that my fiancé will be put off by them.'

'No problem,' says dad, 'All you have to do is wash your feet as often as possible and always wear socks, even to bed.'

The bride-to-be goes to her mom for help, 'Mom,' she says, 'When I wake up in the morning, my breath is awful.'

'Try this in the morning – get straight out of bed, go to the kitchen to make breakfast. While he is busy eating, brush your teeth. Don't say a word until you've brushed your teeth.'

The couple marry and all is fine until one day the husband wakes with a start to find one of his socks had come off. Fearful of the consequences, he frantically searches the bed. This, of course, wakes his bride and with without thinking breathes over him and asks, 'Honey, what are you looking for?'

'Oh no,' he replies. 'You must have swallowed my sock!'

The milkman:

I said to the wife, 'Guess what I heard down at the pub? They reckon the milkman has made love to every woman in our street except one.'

She replied, 'I'll bet it's that stuck-up Phyllis at number 25.'

Sued Hospital:

A recent article in the West Australian newspaper reported that a woman was suing a Perth Hospital, saying that after her husband had surgery, he had lost all interest in sex.

A hospital spokesman replied: 'Mr. Maynard was admitted for cataract surgery. All we did was correct his eyesight.'

Making whoopee:

- An Irishman was walking home late at night and sees a woman in the dark shadows.

    'Twenty pounds,' she whispers.

    Murphy had never been with a hooker before, but decides what the hell, it's only twenty pounds. So they hid in the bushes.

    They're going 'at it' for a minute when all of a sudden a light flashes on them. It is a Police Officer.

    'Allo, Allo, Allo, What's going on here, people?' asks the cop.

    'Ta be shure, O'im making love to me missus,' Paddy answers sounding annoyed.

    'Oh, I'm sorry,' says the cop, 'I didn't know.'

    'Well, neidder did I, til ya shined that bloody light in her face!'

- Paddy says to Mick 'I found this pen. Is it yours?'

    Mick replies 'Don't know, give it here.' He then tries it by writing a few words on a piece of paper and says, 'Yes it is'

Paddy asks 'How do you know?'

Mick replies, 'That's my handwriting.'

- Compromising does not mean you are wrong and your wife is right. It only means that your survival instinct is stronger than your ego!

- A woman loses both ears in an accident. A plastic surgeon she consults tells her that ear transplants are still in the testing stage, but he will do what he can. The woman undergoes the operation, and after a time she returns to the surgeon's office to have the bandages removed and the stitches taken out. After examining her, the doctor tells her everything seems to have gone well, and she seems pleased with his work.

  The next day, however, she calls the plastic surgeon in a rage. 'You know what you did?' she screams. 'You gave me a man's ears.'

  'Well,' says the surgeon, 'an ear is an ear. What's wrong? Can't you hear?'

  'I hear everything,' she says. 'The problem is I don't understand anything I'm told.'

- A mortician was working late one night. He examined the body of Mr. Schwartz, about to be cremated, and made a startling discovery. Schwartz had the largest private part he had ever seen!

  'I'm sorry Mr. Schwartz,' the mortician commented, 'I can't allow you to be cremated with such an impressive private part. It must be saved for posterity.'

  So, he removed it, stuffed it into his briefcase, and took it home.

  'I have something to show you won't believe,' he said to his wife, opening his briefcase.

  'My God!' the wife exclaimed, 'Schwartz is dead!'

- My husband got so excited when I told him I had bought him SUV for Christmas. After he rang all his mates to tell them, it was so funny when I told him it was socks, undies and Viagra.

Inter-galactic travel:

The year is 2222 and Mike and Maureen land on Mars after accumulating enough frequent flier miles. They meet a Martian couple and are talking about all sorts of things.

Mike asks if Mars has a stock market, if they have laptop computers, how they make money, etc.

Finally, Maureen brings up the subject of sex.

'Just how do you guys do it?' asks Maureen.

'Pretty much the way you do,' responds the Martian.

Discussion ensues and finally the couples decide to swap partners for the night and experience one another.

Maureen and the male Martian go off to a bedroom where the Martian strips. He's got only a teeny, weeny member about half an inch long and just a quarter inch thick.

'I don't think this is going to work,' says Maureen.

'Why?' he asks, 'What's the matter?'

'Well,' she replies, 'It's just not long enough to reach me!'

'No problem,' he says, and proceeds to slap his forehead with his palm. With each slap of his forehead, his member grows until it's quite impressively long.

'Well,' she says, 'That's quite impressive, but it's still pretty narrow.'

'No problem,' he says, and starts pulling his ears. With each pull, his member grows wider and wider until the entire measurement is extremely exciting to the woman.

'Wow!' she exclaims, as they fell into bed and made mad, passionate love.

The next day the couples re-join their normal partners and go their separate ways.

As they walk along, Mike asks 'Well, was it any good?'

'I hate to say it,' says Maureen, 'but it was pretty wonderful. How about you?'

'It was horrible,' he replies, All I got was a headache. All she kept doing the whole time was slapping my forehead and pulling my ears.'

Playing Doctor:

Two married men are in a pub discussing their love life when one says, 'Have you ever tried playing doctor?'

His buddy says, 'No. What's it like?'

The man replies, 'It's amazing. Me and my wife were playing for about 10 hours.'

His buddy, shocked says, '10 hours!? How the hell did you manage that long?'

'I just left her in the waiting room for nine and a half hours.'

The Confession:

Hi Bob,

This is Alan next door. I'm sorry buddy, but I have a confession to make to you. I've been riddled with guilt these past few months and have been trying to pluck up the courage to tell you to your face, but I am at least now telling in text as I can't live with myself a moment longer without you knowing. The truth is I have been sharing your wife, day and night when you're not around. In fact, probably more than you. I haven't been getting it at home recently, but that's no excuse, I know. The temptation was just too much. I can no longer live with the guilt and I hope you will accept my sincerest apologies and forgive me. I promise that it won't happen again. Please come up with a fee for usage, and I'll pay you.

Regards, Alan.

The Actions:

Bob, feeling insulted and betrayed, grabbed his gun, and shot his neighbour dead. He returned home where he poured himself a stiff drink and sat down on the sofa. He took out his phone where he saw he has a subsequent message from his neighbour:

The Second Message

Hi Bob,

This is Alan next door again. Sorry about the slight typo on my last text. I expect you worked it out anyway, but as I'm sure you noticed that my Autocorrect changed 'Wi-Fi' To 'Wife'. Technology hey?!? Hope you saw the funny side of that.

Regards, Alan

The Arousal:

After 20 years of marriage, a couple was lying in bed one evening, when the wife felt her husband begin to fondle her in ways he hadn't in quite some time. It almost tickled as his fingers started at her neck, and then began moving down past the small of her back. He then caressed her shoulders and neck, slowly worked his hand down over her breasts, stopping just over her lower stomach. He then proceeded to place his hand on her left inner arm, caressed past the side of her breast again, working down her side, passed gently over her buttock and down her leg to her calf. Then, he proceeded up her inner thigh, stopping just at the uppermost portion of her leg.

He continued in the same manner on her right side, then suddenly stopped, rolled over and started to watch TV. As she had become quite aroused by this caressing, she asked in a loving voice, 'That was wonderful. Why did you stop?'

He said, 'I found the remote.'

I need help!

A hotel guest calls the Front desk and the clerk answers, 'May I help you, sir?'

The man says, 'Yes, I'm in room 858. You need to send someone to my room immediately. I'm having an argument with my wife and she says she's going to jump out the window.'

The desk clerk says, 'I'm sorry sir, but that's a personal matter.'

The man replies, 'Listen you idiot. The window won't open... that's a maintenance matter.'

Simple Truths

Simple truth #1:

Lovers help each other undress before sex. However, after sex, they always dress on their own.

Moral of the story - In life, no one helps you once you've been screwed.

Simple truth #2:

When a lady is pregnant, all her friends touch the stomach and say, 'Congrats.' But, none of them comes up to the man - touches his penis and say, 'Good job.'

Moral of the story - Hard work is rarely appreciated.

Trying it out:

A senior couple decides to try routine Viagra for the first time ever. They have an incredible night together.

In the morning, the wife asks her husband at breakfast time, 'Would you like some bacon and eggs, a slice of toast, and maybe some grapefruit juice and coffee?'

He declines. 'Thanks for asking, but, I'm not hungry right now. It's this Viagra,' he says. 'It's really taken the edge off my appetite.'

At lunchtime, she asks him if he'd like something. 'How about a bowl of soup, homemade muffins, or a cheese sandwich?'

He declines. 'The Viagra,' he says, 'really trashes my desire for food.'

Come dinner time, she asks if he wants anything to eat. 'Would you like a juicy rib eye steak and some scrumptious apple pie? Or maybe a rotisserie chicken or tasty stir fry?'

He declines again. 'No,' he says, 'it's got to be the Viagra. I'm still not hungry.'

'Well,' she says, 'Would you mind letting me up? I'm starving!'

Water in the carburettor:

Wife: 'There is trouble with the car. It has water in the carburettor.'

Husband: 'Water in the carburettor? That's ridiculous!'

Wife: 'I tell you the car has water in the carburettor.'

Husband: 'You don't even know what a carburettor is. I'll check it out. Where's the car?

Wife: 'In the pool.'

Birthday gift:

For her birthday, Jimmy thought it would be nice to buy his wife a little gift. Always short of money, he thought long and hard about what that present might be. Unable to decide, Jimmy entered the cosmetics section and asked the girl, 'How about some perfume?'

She showed him a bottle costing $150.

'Too expensive, muttered Jimmy.

The young lady returned with a smaller bottle for $50.

'Oh dear,' Jimmy growled, 'still far too much.'

Growing rather annoyed at Jimmy's meanness, the sales girl brought out a tiny $10 bottle and offered it to him.

Jimmy became really agitated. 'What I mean,' he whined, 'is I'd like to see something really cheap.'

So the sales girl handed him a mirror.

Other birthday gifts:

- Ole bought Lena a piano for her birthday. A few weeks later, Lars inquired how she was doing with it.

   'Oh' said Ole, 'I persvaded her to svitch to a clarinet.'

   'How come?' asked Lars.

   'Vell,' Ole answered, 'because vith a clarinet, she can't sing.'

- A man gave his wife a diamond necklace for their anniversary and his wife didn't speak to him for six months.

   His friend asks, 'Why? Was the necklace a fake?'

   'Nooooo,' he replied. 'That was the deal...'

Christmas gift:

A guy bought his wife a beautiful diamond ring for Christmas. After hearing about this extravagant gift, a friend of his said, 'I thought she wanted one of those sporty four-wheel-drive vehicles.'

'She did,' he replied, 'but where was I going to find a fake Jeep?'

Going home to Mother:

Married man watching his wife packing her clothes says, 'Where are you going?'

'I'm moving in with my mother.'

The husband starts packing his clothes and his wife asks, 'Now where are you going?'

Husband replies, 'I'm also moving in with my mother.'

Wife enquires, 'And what about the kids?'

Husband replies, 'Well I guess ... If you're moving to your mother's and I'm moving to my mother's ... they should move in with their mother.'

Cheating spouse:

A woman was sure that her husband was cheating on her by having an affair with the maid, so she laid down a trap. One evening, she sent the maid home for the weekend and didn't tell her husband.

That night when they went to bed, the husband gave the old story: 'Excuse me my dear, my stomach aches,' and went to the bathroom.

The wife promptly went and got into the maid's bed. She switched off the lights. When he came in silently, he wasted no time or words but had his way with her. When he finished and was still panting, the wife said, 'You didn't expect to find me in this bed, did you?'

He replied, 'No ma'am.'

When she stitched on the light she saw that it was their gardener.

Important Definitions:

No dictionary has ever been able to satisfactorily define the difference between the words *'complete'* and *'finished.'* However, during a recent linguistic conference held in London, and attended by some of the best linguists in the world, Samsundar Balgobin, a Guyanese linguist, was the presenter when he was asked to make that very distinction.

The question put to him by a colleague in the erudite audience was this: 'Some say there is no difference between 'complete' and 'finished.' Please explain the difference in a way that is easy to understand.

Mr. Balgobins response was: 'When you marry the right woman, you are complete. If you marry the wrong woman, you are finished. And, if the right one catches you with the wrong one, you are completely finished.

The distinction between Guts and Balls: To those of you who are nit-pickers about the meaning of words: there is a medical distinction between guts and balls. We've all heard about people having guts or balls, but do you really know the difference between them? In an effort to keep you informed, here are the definitions:

Guts: Is arriving home late, after a night out with the guys, being met by your wife with a broom, and having the guts to ask, 'Are you still cleaning, or are you flying off somewhere?'

Balls: Is coming home late after a night out with the guys, smelling of perfume and beer, with lipstick on your collar and slapping your wife on the bum and having the balls to say, 'You're next, Chubby.'

I hope this clears up any confusion on the definitions. Medically speaking, there is no difference in the outcome – both result in death.

Glasses don't work:

Woman to optometrist: 'I'm returning these glasses I bought for my husband. He's still not seeing things my way.'

The funeral

His wife's graveside service was just barely finished when there was a tremendous bolt of lightning, followed by a massive clap of thunder, accompanied by even more thunder rumbling in the distance.

The little old man looked at the pastor and calmly said, 'Well, she's there.'

Frustration

A frustrated husband in front of his laptop:

'Dear google, please do not behave like my wife... Please allow me to complete my sentence before you start guessing and suggesting...'

A married man's prayer:

Dear God, U gave me childhood, U took it away; U gave me youth, U took it away; U gave me a wife.......... It's been years now, just reminding U.......

The lion:

Employee: 'Sir, you are like a lion in the office. What about at home?'

Boss: 'I am a lion at home too, but there we have a lion tamer.'

CHAPTER 2

MALE JOKES

Sex at 66:

I just took a leaflet out of my mailbox informing me that I can have sex at 66. I'm so happy, because I live at number 64. So it's not too far to walk home afterwards. And it's the same side of the street. I don't even have to cross the road!

Pleasing a woman:

When I was a child, I remember my Mom telling me, 'Son, when you grow up, you can marry any girl you please.'

When I became a young man, I learned the sad fact was that I could not please any of them.

After the vasectomy:

'I thought my vasectomy would keep my wife from getting pregnant but apparently it just changes the colour of the baby.'

Relationship tip for men:

When a woman says, 'Correct me if I'm wrong but … 'Don't do it! It's a trap! Do NOT, I repeat, do NOT correct the woman!'

Spring:

A time when a young man's fancy turns to beer, boats and broads.

Using drugs:

I think it's just terrible and disgusting how everyone has treated Lance Armstrong, especially after what he achieved – winning seven Tour de France races – while on drugs.

When I was on drugs, I couldn't even find my bike let alone ride it.

Prostate exam:

After my prostate exam, the doctor left. When the nurse came in, she whispered the four words no man wants to hear, 'Who was that man?'

Keeping him busy:

Jack goes to his friend Mike and says, 'I'm sleeping with the pastor's wife. Can you hold him in church for an hour after services for me?'

The friend doesn't like it, but being a friend, he agrees. After the services, he starts talking to the pastor, asking him all sorts of stupid questions, just to keep him occupied.

Finally, the pastor gets annoyed and asks Mike what he's really up to. Mike, feeling guilty, finally confesses to the pastor, 'My friend is sleeping with your wife right now, so he asked me to keep you occupied.'

The pastor smiles, puts a brotherly hand on Mike's shoulder and says, 'You'd better hurry home, my wife died a year ago.'

Needlework:

Angus from Glasgow went to a neighbour exclaiming, 'Maggie, cud ya be sewin on a wee button that's come of me fly? I canna button me pants.'

'Oh Angus, I've got me hands in the dishpan. Go next door and see if Mrs. MacDonald could be helpin ya with it.'

About five minutes later, there's a terrible crash and bang next door; a bit of yelling and the sounds of a body falling down stairs.

Walking back into Maggie's back door with a blackened eye and a bloody nose came Angus. Maggie looks at him and says, 'My God, what happened to ya? Did you ask her like I told ya?'

'Aye,' says Angus. 'I askd her to sew on the wee button and she did. Everyting was goin' fine, but when she bent doon to bite off the wee thread, Mr. MacDonald walked in.'

This 'N That:

- I lost a good friend and drinking mate this past weekend at a tragic accident – he got his finger caught in a wedding ring.
- Wanted: a tall girl with good reputation who can cook frog legs and who can stand a little future fun at selected parties and frolicking without getting sick.
- Two bachelors were talking about their respective choice of life partner. One friend said, 'It's generally said that people with opposite characteristics make the happiest marriages. What's your opinion?'
  The friend replied, 'Yes, they are right. That's why I'm looking for a gal with money!'
- A bloke was sitting in the front row at the Rugby World Cup Finals, but amazingly, there was an empty seat beside him. Another man spots it, goes up to him and says, 'Do you mind if I sit here?'
  'No, not at all,' replies the first man. 'It's my wife's seat, but she died recently.'
  'So why didn't you get one of your family to come?' asks the second man out of curiosity.
  'They're all at the funeral.'
- A ladies' man stops for the night at a country hotel and as he signs in, notices a beautiful blonde sitting alone at the bar. While the receptionist is sorting out te paperwork, he saunters over to the blonde and returns a couple of minutes later with her on his arm.
  Grinning, he says to the receptionist, 'Would you believe it! I've just bumped into my wife, so we'd better have a double room.'
  The next morning, he goes to pay his bill and sees it's more than $2,000.'

'What the Hell's this for?' he sputters. 'I've only been here one night.'

'Of course sir, but your wife has been here for more than a week!'

- Two guys are drinking in a bar. One says, 'My wife ran off with my best friend.'

  His drinking companion says, 'I thought I was your best friend.'

  'Not any more,' was the reply.

- Best Slogan on a man's T-Shirt:

  'Please Do Not Disturb me, I'm married and already very disturbed.'

Man, you look tired!

I couldn't help but overhear two blokes in their mid-twenties while sitting at the bar last night. One of the guys says to his mate: 'Man you look tired.'

His mate says: 'Man I'm exhausted. My girlfriend and I have sex all the time. She's after me three and four times a day. I just don't know what to do.'

Sitting a couple of stools down, two men overheard the conversation. One of them looked over at the two young men and with the wisdom of years says, 'Marry her – that will put a stop to that.'

Golfing:

A young man who was also an avid golfer found himself with a few hours to spare one afternoon. He figured if he hurried and played very fast, he could get in nine holdes before he had to go home.

Just as he was about to tee off, an old gentleman shuffled onto the tee and asked if he could accompany the young man as he was golfing alone. Not being able to say no, he allowed the old gent to join him. To his surprise, the old man played fairly quickly. He didn't hit the ball far, but plodded along consistently and didn't waste much time.

Finally, they reached the ninth fairway and the young man found himself with a tough shot. There was a large pine tree right in front of his ball, and directly between his ball and the green. After several minutes of debating how to hit the shot, the old man finally said, 'You know, when I was your age I'd hit the ball right over that tree.'

With that challenge placed before him, the young man swung hard, hit the ball up right smack into the top of the tree trunk and it thudded back on the ground not a foot from where it had originally lay.

The old man offered one more comment, 'Of course, when I was your age, that pine tree was only three feet tall.'

Italian mother:

Giuseppe excitedly tells his mother he's fallen in love and that he's going to get married.

He says, 'Just for fun, Mama, I'm going to bring over three women and you try and guess which one I'm going to marry.'

The mother agrees. The next day, he brings three beautiful women into the house, sits them down on the couch and they chat for a while. After the women leave, he then says, 'Okay, Mama, guess which one I'm going to marry?'

Mom identifies the one she thinks he will marry.

'That's amazing, Mama. You're right. How did you know?'

Mama replies: 'I don't like her.'

Dinner guest:

A man brings his best buddy home for dinner unannounced at 5:30 after work.

His wife begins screaming at him and his friend just sits and listens in.

'My hair and makeup are not done, the house is a mess, the dishes are not done. I'm still in my pyjamas and I can't be bothered with cooking tonight. What the hell did you bring him home for?'

Husband answers: 'Because he's thinking of getting married.'

Louiggi:

Luiggi walks to work 20 blocks every day and passes a shoe store twice every day. Each day he stops and looks in the window to admire the Armani leather shoes. He wants those shoes so much – it's all he can think about. After about two months he saves the price of the shoes, $300, and purchases them.

Every Friday night the Italian community holds a dance in the church basement. Luiggi seizes this opportunity to wear his new Armani leather shoes for the first time. He asks Sophia to dance and as they dance he asks her, 'Sophia, do you wear red panties tonight?'

Startled, Sophia replies, 'Yes, Luiggi, I do wear red panties tonight, but how do you know?'

Luiggi answers, 'I see the reflection in my new $300 Armani leather shoes. How do you like them?'

Next he asks Rosa to dance, and after a few minutes he asks, 'Rosa, do you wear white panties tonight?'

Rosa answers, 'Yes, Luiggi, I do, but how do you know that?'

He replies, 'I see the reflection in my new $300 Armani leather shoes. How do you like them?'

Now as the evening is almost over and the last song is being played, Luiggi asks Carmela to dance.

Midway through the dance his face turns red. He states, 'Carmela, be stilla my heart, please, please tell me you wear no panties tonight. Please, please, tella me this true!'

Carmela smiles coyly and answers, 'Yes Luiggi, I wear no panties tonight.'

Luiggi gasps, 'Thanka God – I thought I had a crack in my $300 Armani leather shoes!

CHAPTER 3

FEMALES

Jewish mother:

The year is 2016 and the United States has elected the first woman as well as the first Jewish president, Susan Goldfarb. She calls up her mother a few weeks after Election Day and says, 'So, Mom, I assume you'll be coming to my inauguration?'

'I don't think so. It's a ten-hour drive, your father isn't as young as he used to be, and my arthritis is acting up again.'

'Don't worry about it Mom, I'll send Air Force One to pick you up and take you home. And a limousine will pick you up at your door.'

''I don't know. Everybody will be so fancy-schmantzy, what on earth would I wear?'

Susan replies, 'I'll make sure you have a wonderful gown custom-made by the best designer in New York.'

''Honey,' Mom complains, 'you know I can't eat those rich foods you and your friends like to eat.'

The President-to-be responds, 'Don't worry Mom. The entire affair is going to be handled by the best caterer in New York, kosher all the way. Mom, I really want you to come.'

So Mom reluctantly agrees and on January 20, 2017, Susan Goldfarb is being sworn in as President of the United States. In the front row sits the new President's mother, who leans over to a senator sitting next to her and says, 'You see that woman over there with her hand on the Torah, becoming President of the United States?'

The Senator whispers back, 'Yes I do.'

Mom says proudly, 'Her brother is a doctor.'

Mine's the best!

Three women who were friends in high school have returned to their hometown to attend their 25th reunion and have lunch together. Their talk turns to their position in life, and it's clear that they're trying to one-up each other.

The first woman says, 'My husband is taking me to the French Riviera for two weeks,' and then looks at the others with a superior demeanour.

The second woman says, 'Well, my husband just bought me a new Mercedes,' and looks about with considerable pride.

The third woman says, 'Well, to be perfectly honest with you, we don't have much money and we don't have any material possessions - but 13 canaries can stand shoulder to shoulder on my husband's erect penis.'

After a long silence, the first woman looks shame-faced and says, 'Girls, I've got a confession to make. I was just trying to impress you. We're not really going to the French Riviera. We're going to my parent's house for two weeks.'

The second woman says, 'Your honesty has shamed me. To be honest, my husband didn't buy me a Mercedes - he bought me a Taurus.'

'Well,' the third woman says, 'I also have a confession to make. Canary number 13 has to stand on one leg.'

To get to Heaven:

God visited a woman and told her she must give up smoking, drinking and sex if she wants to get into Heaven. The woman said she would try her best.

God visited the woman a week later to see how she was getting on.

'Not bad,' said the woman, 'I've given up smoking and drinking, but when I bent over the lounge suite and my boyfiend caught sight of my long slender legs, he made love to me right then and there.'

'They don't like that in heaven' said God.

The woman replied: 'They're not too happy about it at Harvey Norman either!'

Tattoo:

My daughter suggested that I get the names of my children tattooed on my body. I told her I already did... they're called stretch marks.

Wonder Woman:

I may not be Wonder Woman, but I can do things that make you wonder.

Young bride:

Sarah, a new young bride, calls her mother in tears. She sobs, 'Harry doesn't appreciate what I do for him.'

'Now, now,' her mother comforted, 'I'm sure it was all just a misunderstanding.'

'No, mother, you don't understand. I bought a frozen turkey roll and he yelled and screamed at me about the price,'

'Well the nerve of that lousy cheapskate,' says her mom. 'Those turkey rolls are only a few dollars.'

'No, mother, it wasn't the price of the turkey. It was the price of the plane ticket.'

'Plane ticket? What did you need an airplane ticket for?'

'Well mother, when I went to fix it, I looked at the directions on the package and it said: *Prepare from a frozen state,* so I flew to Alaska.'

Fortune Teller:

A long-suffering country wife decided to go and see a fortune teller when she was at the local show. In a dark tent, peering into a crystal ball, the mystic delivered some grave news. 'There's no easy way to say this, so I'll just be blunt,' she said. 'Prepare yourself to be a widow. Your husband will die a violent and horrible death this year.'

Visibly shaken, the woman stared at the fortune teller, took a few deep breaths to compose herself and said, 'I have to know – will I be acquitted?'

New title:

Instead of giving 'single' as a status – I prefer 'independently owned and operated!'

CHAPTER 4

LAWYERS

True Story:

This actually took place in Charlotte, North Carolina.

A lawyer purchased a box of very rare and expensive cigars, then insured them against, among other things, fire. Within a month, having smoked his entire stockpile of these cigars, the lawyer filed a claim against the insurance company. In his claim the lawyer stated the cigars were lost 'in a series of small fires.'

The insurance company refused to pay, citing the obvious reason, that the man had consumed the cigars in the normal fashion.

The lawyer sued and won!

(Stay with me now ...)

Delivering the ruling, the judge agreed with the insurance company that the claim was frivolous. The judge stated nevertheless, that the lawyer held a policy from the company, in which it had warranted that the cigars were insurable and also guaranteed that it would insure them against fire, without defining what is considered to be unacceptable 'fire' and was obligated to pay the claim.

Rather than endure lengthy and costly appeal process, the insurance company accepted the ruling and paid $15,000 to the lawyer for his loss of the cigars that perished in the 'fires'.

Now for the best part...

After the lawyer cashed the check, the insurance company had him arrested on twenty-four counts of arson! With his own insurance claim and testimony from the previous case being used against him, the lawyer was convicted of intentionally burning his insured property and was sentenced to twenty-four months in jail and a $24,000 fine.

This true story won first place in last year's Criminal Lawyers Award contest.

Only in America!

Good and bad news:

A lawyer calls his largest client to his office for an important meeting. When he arrives, the lawyer says to the wealthy art collector client, 'I have some good news and some bad news.'

The client grumbles, 'I've had an awful day. Tell me the good news first.'

'Your wife invested $5,000 in two pictures today. She believes they are worth at least $3 million.'

'Well done!' the tycoon says with a big smile.

'Good news indeed! You've made my day. So what's the bad news?'

'The two pictures are of you with your secretary.'

Rental Home:

A lawyer had a wife and twelve children and needed to move as his rental agreement was coming to an end for the home where he lived but was having difficulty in finding a new home.

When he said he had twelve children, no one would rent a home to him because they knew that the children would likely destroy the home. He could not say that he had no children, and decided he could not lie, (after all, lawyers cannot and do not lie.)

So, he had an idea. He sent his wife for a walk to the cemetery with eleven of their children. He took the remaining child with him to see homes with the real estate agent.

He liked one of the homes and the agent asked: 'How many children do you have?'

He answered: 'Twelve children.'

The agent asked: 'Where are the others?'

The lawyer answered, with a sad look, 'They're in the cemetery with their mother'

And that's the way he was able to rent a home for his family without lying.

Moral: It is not necessary to lie, one only has to choose the right words. Lawyers don't lie... they're just very creative.

Three choices:

A housewife, an accountant and a lawyer are asked, 'How much is 2 + 2?'

The housewife replies, 'Four.'

The accountant replies: 'I think it's either three or four - let me run those figures through my calculator.'

The lawyer pulls the drapes, dims the lights and asks in a hushed voice, 'How much do you want it to be?'

Politcs:

- Politics is the art of looking for trouble, finding it everywhere, diagnosing it incorrectly, and applying the wrong remedies.
- Man conducting an opinion poll: 'What should we do with people who rely on government handouts, but are too lazy to work.'
  Woman homeowner, 'Kick them out of parliament.'
- Instead of giving politicians the keys to the city, it might be better to change the locks.
- When you go into court, you are putting yourself in the hands of twelve people, none of whom were smart enough to get out of jury duty.

- A fine is a tax for doing wrong. A tax is a fine for doing well.

The engineer:

An engineer dies and reports to the Pearly Gates. Saint Peter checks his dossier and not seeing his name there, accidentally sends him to Hell. It doesn't take long before the engineer becomes rather dissatisfied with the level of comfort in Hell.

He soon begins to design and build improvements. Shortly thereafter, Hell has air conditioning, flush toilets and escalators. Needless to say, the engineer is a very popular man.

One day, God calls Satan and says, 'So, how are things in Hell?'

Satan replies, 'Hey, things are going great. We've got air conditioning, flush toilets and escalators. And there's no telling what this engineer is going to come up with next.'

'What!' exclaims God, 'You've got an engineer? That's a mistake – he should never have been sent to Hell. Send him to me.'

'Not a chance,' Satan replies, 'I like having an engineer on the staff – so I'm keeping him!'

God insists: 'Send him back or I'll sue.'

Satan laughs uproariously and answers, 'Yeah. Right. And where are you going to get a lawyer?'

CHAPTER 5

DOCTORS

Dying soldier:

A highly decorated veteran soldier was dying in a hospital and asked the priest to call a bureaucrat and a politician. Within minutes, the two appeared. He asked them to sit on either side of the bed.

The priest held their hands and kept quiet.

The guys were so touched and at the same time felt very important for being summoned by a highly decorated war veteran in his dying moment.

Out of anxiety, the politician asked, 'But why did you call us?'

The soldier gathered all his strength and said, 'Jesus died between two thieves and I want to go the same way!'

This will explain the true meaning of a positive attitude:

Late in the night he regained consciousness. He found himself in agonizing pain in the hospital ICU, with tubes up his nose, wires monitoring every function and a gorgeous nurse hovering over him. He realized he'd obviously been in a serious accident.

She gave him a deep look straight into the eyes, and he heard her slowly say, 'You may not feel anything from the waist down.'

Somehow he managed to mumble in reply, 'Can I feel your boobs, then?'

That, my friends, is a positive attitude!

The clinic:

A doctor in Dublin wanted to get off work and go fishing, so he approached his assistant: 'Murphy, I'm going fishing tomorrow and don't want to close the clinic. I want you to take care of the clinic and take care of all me patients.'

'Yes, sir!' answers Murphy.

The doctor goes fishing and returns the following day and asks: 'So, Murphy, how was your day?'

Murphy told him that he took care of three patients. 'The first one had a headache so I gave him Paracetamol.'

'Bravo Murphy lad, and the second one?' asks the doctor.

'The second one had indigestion and I gave him Gaviscon.' says Murphy.

'Bravo, bravo! You're good at this and what about the third one?' asks the doctor.

'Sir, I was sitting here and suddenly the door flies open and a young gorgeous woman bursts in so she does. Like a bolt outta the blue, she tears off her clothes, taking off everyting including her bra and her knickers and lies down on the table, spreading her legs and shouts: 'Help me for the love of St Patrick! For five years I have not seen a man!'

'Tunderin' lard Jesus Murphy, what did you do?' asks the doctor.

'I put drops in her eyes.'

What your body does in a day:

Sometimes you may feel like your body is beginning to creak and fail you on the outside, but do you ever stop to consider the incredible work that is taking place inside of it? There is so much going on and everything fits together so well, that it's almost impossible to comprehend it. The following will remind you that there are miracles going on inside your body every single day.

- Your heart pumps approximately 7,571 litres of blood through its chambers every single day. It beats more than 100,000 times a day to achieve this incredible feat.

- Red blood cells literally shoot around the body, taking less than 60 seconds to complete a full circuit. This means that each of your blood cells take 1,440 trips around your body every day, delivering oxygen and keeping your body energized. Each cell lives for about 40 days, before being replaced by a younger model. It's no surprise their life span is short, having made 60,000 trips around the body – they must be exhausted!
- You take around 17,000 breaths a day on average, and don't have to think about a single one of them. Yet if you want to stop breathing temporarily, you can voluntarily hold your breath. A typical pair of adult lungs can hold a huge six litres of air.
- Every day, your body ensures that you don't contact cancer thousands of times over. Cancer is formed when cells are altered in a way which re-programs their DNA and it's estimated that tens of thousands of cells suffer cancer-causing lesions every day. But the body sends special enzymes scuttling around to inspect DNA strands for faults and fixes them before they turn into tumours.
- Your brain doesn't stop working. It's estimated that about 50,000 thoughts pass through it each day on average, although some scientists put the figure closer to 60,000. That is a whopping 35-48 thoughts every minute.
- The cells in your stomach lining produce an alkaline substance every few milliseconds to neutralize stomach acid. If they didn't do this, your stomach would digest itself, because some of the acids are strong enough to dissolve metals. Your stomach has to produce a new layer of mucus every two weeks otherwise it will digest itself.
- Your body works overtime to digest your food and the process starts before it even hits the mouth. When you smell food, your mouth automatically produces more saliva to prepare the digestive system for work. It takes

about 6-8 hours for food to pass through the stomach and two days to complete the digestion process. The average person will eat over 50 tonnes of food in his or her lifetime, which seems ridiculous!
- The glands in your mouth produce an incredible 1.5 litres of saliva every day. That's a lot of dribble! If this didn't happen, your mouth would dry up and become overrun with bacteria and you wouldn't be able to digest your food.
- You blink about 28,000 times every day, with each one lasting just a tenth of a second. This is a voluntary reflex the body uses to keep the eyes clean and moist, which is pretty crucial given that 90% of the information you process is visual, and you can weigh up any visual scene in just 0.01 seconds. Consider how many people and objects you look at every day – it's remarkable!
- Most of the body's energy is expelled via heat. Your body produces the same heat as 25 watt light bulbs over the course of a single day.
- You shed more than one million skin cells every single day but they are constantly replenished automatically, to save you from turning transparent and becoming rather exposed! Your skin is actually an organ; in fact, it's the largest organ you have, with a surface area of 18 square feet (2 square metres).
- Your hair (if you still have any) grows about half a millimetre per day, and the average adult with a full scalp has around 100,000 hairs on their head. So that's a combined 50 metres of hair growth every single day.
- Your liver is so busy over the course of a day, it's almost impossible to summarize its activities. It manufactures cholesterol, vitamin D and blood plasma; it identifies the nutrients your body needs, and stores some away for future use; it filters 1.43 litres of blood every minute and produces .94 litres of bile every day to help to break down your food. Basically, you have a

factory plant running inside you every day, which is pretty amazing!
- Each of your kidneys contains 1 million tiny filters that work together to filter an average of 1.3 litres of blood every minute – that's 1,872 litres every single day, despite each kidney only being the size of a fist. If that wasn't enough, they also expel an average of 1.4 litres of urine from your body every day too.
- The average male's testicles manufacture 10 million new sperm cells every day. Those that aren't used age and are eventually broken down inside the body with any useful nutrients being absorbed and put to use.
- You grow 8mm every night while sleeping, before shrinking back down again the next day. This saves you from some pretty hefty clothing bills and ensures you don't have to raise the door frames in your home every year or two.
- And almost amazing of all, your body cells are regenerating themselves every single day without any prompting. This means you have an entirely new set of taste buds every ten days, new nails every 6-10 months, new bones every ten years and even a new heart every 20 years.

So next time you think that your body is starting to creak, just think about all the incredible things that are happening inside it every day, because all of us really are a miracle!

Just old age:

An elderly bloke went to his young doctor complaining of a terrible pain in his leg.

'I am afraid it's just old age,' replied his doctor. 'There is nothing we can do about it.'

'That can't be,' fumed the patient. 'You don't know what you're doing.'

'How can you possibly think I am wrong?' countered the doctor.

'Well, it's perfectly obvious,' the old man replied. 'My other leg is fine, and it's the exact same age!'

Sleeping pills:

Doctor: 'Madam, your husband needs rest and peace, so here are some sleeping pills.'

Wife: 'Doc when should I give them to him?'

Doctor: 'They're for you!'

The speaker:

A dinner speaker was in such a hurry to get to his engagement that when he arrived and visited the men's room, he suddenly realized that he had forgotten his false teeth.

Turning to the man next to him he said, 'I forgot my teeth.'

The man said, 'No problem,' He reached into his pocket and pulled out a pair of false teeth. 'Try these,' he said.'

The speaker tried them. 'Too loose.'

The man then said, 'I have another pair, try these.'

The speaker tried them and responded, 'Too tight.'

The man was not taken back at all and replied, 'I have one more pair. Try them.'

The speaker said, 'They fit perfectly.'

With that, he ate his meal and gave his speech. After the dinner meeting was over, the speaker went over to thank the man who had helped him. 'I want to thank you for coming to my aid. Where is your office? I've been looking for a good dentist.'

The man replied, 'I'm not a dentist. I'm an undertaker.'

(Oh – that's gross!)

Hypochondriac:

Brian, one of the world's greatest hypochondriacs, bumped into his doctor one day at the supermarket.

'Doc!' Brian exclaimed, 'I've been meaning to tell you; remember those voices I kept on hearing in my head? I haven't heard them in over a week!'

'Wow! What wonderful news Brian! I'm so happy for you!' his doctor exclaimed.

'Wonderful?' asked a dismal-looking Brian. 'There's nothing wonderful about it. I'm afraid my hearing is starting to go!'

Group therapy session:

A psychiatrist was conducting a group therapy session with five young mothers and their small children.

'You all have obsessions,' the psychiatrist stated. 'I'm concerned that these individual obsessions are going to impact upon your children.'

To the first mother, Mary, he said, 'You are obsessed with eating. You've even named your daughter Candy.'

He turned to the second mom, Ann: 'Your obsession is with money. It manifests itself in your children's names; Penny, Goldie and Frank.'

He turned to the third mom, Joyce, 'Your obsession is alcohol. This too shows itself in your children's names; Brandy and Sherry. You've even called your cat Whisky.'

He then turned to the fourth mom, June, 'Your obsession is with flowers. Your girls are called Rose, Daphne and Poppy.'

At this point, the fifth mother, Kathy, quietly got up, took her little boy by the hand and whispered, 'Come on Dick, this guy has no idea what he's talking about. Grab Fanny and Willy and we're out of here.'

Hair:

The excited man says, 'Doctor, doctor, my hair's coming out. Can you give me something to keep it in?'

'Certainly, how about a paper bag?' he replied.

The cure:

A woman went to the doctor's office where she was seen by one of the younger doctors. After about four minutes in the examination room, she burst out screaming as she ran down the hall.

An older doctor stopped her and asked her what had happened and she told him her story.

After listening, he had her sit down and relax in another room. The older doctor marched down the hallway back to where the young doctor was writing on his clipboard.

'What's the matter with you?' the older doctor demanded. 'Mrs. Terry is 71 years old, has four grown children and seven grandchildren, and you told her she was pregnant?'

The younger doctor continued writing and without looking up said, 'Does she still have the hiccups?'

The best patients:

Five surgeons from big cities discuss who makes the best patients to operate on.

The first surgeon from Melbourne says, 'I like to see accountants on my operating table because when they open them up, everyting inside is numbered.'

The second, from Sydney, responds, 'Yeah, but you should try electricians! Everything inside them is colour coded.'

The third surgeon, from Adelaide says, 'No, I really think librarians are the best – everything inside them is in alphabetical order.'

The fourth surgeon from Perth chimes in, 'You know, I like construction workers. Those guys always understand when you have a few parts left over."

But the fifth surgeon, from Brisbane shut them all up when he observed, 'You're all wrong. Politicians are the easiest to operate on. There are no guts, heart, balls, brains or spine – plus the head and the rear are interchangeable.'

Health Services:

The AMA has weighed in on the proposed changes to Australia's Health Services:

- The Allergists voted to scratch them, but the Dermatologists advised not to make any rash moves.
- The Gastroenterologists had a gut feeling about it, but the Neurologists thought he had a lot of nerve.
- The Obstetricians felt he was labouring under a misconception.
- Opthalmologists considered the ideas short-sighted.
- Pathologists yelled, 'Over my dead body!' while the Paediatricians said, 'Oh, grow up!'
- The psychiatrists thought the ideas were madness while the Radiologists could see right through them.
- The ENT specialists didn't swallow it and just wouldn't hear of it.
- The Pharmacists thought it was a bitter pill to swallow, and the Plastic Surgeons said, 'This puts a whole new face on the matter.'
- The Podiatrists thought it was a step forward, but the Urologists were pissed off at the whole idea.
- The Anaesthetists thought the ideas were a gas, but the Cardiologists didn't have the heart to say no.

In the end, the Proctologists won out, leaving the entire decision up to the arseholes in parliament.

Prostate Exam:

- During my prostate exam I asked the doctor, 'Where should I put my pants?'

  'Over there by mine,' was not the answer I was expecting.

- My husband thinks it is funny to break the tension while having a 'Blokes examination' by telling the doctor, 'Last year the doctor used two fingers; he wanted a second opinion.'

CHAPTER 6

POLICE

Rude driver:

The light turned yellow, just in front of him. He did the right thing and stopped at the crosswalk, even though he could have beaten the red light by accelerating through the intersection.

The tailgating woman behind him was furious and honked her horn, screaming in frustration, as she missed her chance to get through the intersection. As she was still in mid-rant, she heard a tap on her window and looked up into the face of a very serious police officer.

The officer ordered her to exit her car with her hands up. He took her to the police station where she was searched, fingerprinted, photographed and placed in a holding cell. After a couple of hours, a policeman approached the cell and opened the door. She was escorted back to the booking desk where the arresting officer was waiting with her personal effects.

He said, 'I'm very sorry for this mistake. You see, I pulled up behind your car while you were blowing your horn, giving the guy in front of you the finger and cursing at him. I noticed the 'What Would Jesus Do' bumper sticker, the 'Choose Life' license plate holder, the 'Follow Me to Sunday-School' bumper sticker, and the chrome-plated Christian fish emblem on the trunk, so naturally I assumed you had stolen the car.'

Priceless!

If a baby refuses to nap - is that resisting a rest?

The Englishman, the Irishman:

An English man, Scottish man and an Irish man are all waiting their fate on death row.

The Scottish man was asked if he would prefer the guillotine, electric chair or gas chamber.

He chose the guillotine however it stopped an inch from his head so they said he was free to go.

They asked the English man the same question and he chose the guillotine. Again it stopped an inch from his head, they said he was free to go.

The Irish man was asked the same question and he replied that he would prefer the electric chair as the guillotine didn't seem to be working.

The Last Kiss:

Back on June 9th, a group of Illinois bikers were riding west on I-74 when they saw a girl about to jump off the Murray Baker Bridge. So they stopped.

George, their leader, a big burly man of 53, gets off his Harley, walks through a group of gawkers, past the State Trooper who was trying to talk her down off the railing, and says, 'Hey Baby? Whatcha doin' up there on that railin?'

She says tearfully, 'I'm going to commit suicide!'

While he didn't want to appear 'sensitive', George also didn't want to miss this 'be-a-legend' opportunity either so he asked. 'Well, before you jump, Honey-Babe... Why don't you give ole George here your best last kiss?'

So, with no hesitation at all, she leaned back over the railing and did just that... And it was a long, deep, lingering kiss followed immediately by another even better one.

After they breathlessly finished, George gets a big thumbs-up approval from his biker-buddies, the onlookers, and even the State Trooper, and then says, 'Wow! That was the best kiss I have ever had, Honey! That's a real talent you're wasting, Sugar Shorts. You could be famous if you rode with me. Why the hell are you committing suicide?'

'My parents don't like me dressing up like a girl.'

It's still unclear whether he jumped or was pushed.

Groan joke:

A thief in Paris planned to steal some paintings from the Louvre. After careful planning, he got past security, stole the paintings and made it safely to his van. However, he was captured only two blocks away when his van ran out of gas.

When asked how he could mastermind such a crime and then make such an obvious error, he replied, 'Monsieur, that is the reason I stole the paintings.' I had no Monet to buy Degas to make the Van Gogh.'

See if you have De Gaulle to send this on to someone else. I sent it to you because I figured I had nothing Toulouse.

Italian Police:

Five Germans in an Audi Quattro arrive at the Italian border. The Italian Customs Officer stops them and tells them 'Itsa illegal to putta five people in a Quattro.

'Vot do you mean it's illegal?' asks the German driver.

'Quattro meansa four,' replies the Italian official.

'Quattro is just ze name of ze fokken automobile,' the German says unbelievingly.

'Look at ze dam papers: zee car is designed to karry five persons.'

'You canna uulla thata one on m-aa!' replies the customs officer. 'Quattro meansa four. You have five-a people ina your car and thereforea youarra breaking da law.'

The German driver replies angrily, 'You idiot! Call your supervisor over. I vant to speak to someone vis more intelligence!'

'Sorry,' responds the officer, 'He can'ta come. He's busy with two guys in a Fiat Uno.'

Early Shopping:

It was just before Christmas and the magistrate was in a happy mood. He asked the prisoner in the dock, 'What are you charged with?'

The prisoner replied, 'Doing my Christmas shopping early.'

'That's no crime' said the magistrate. 'Just how early were you doing this shopping?'

The prisoner answered, 'Before the store opened.'

Canadian Speed Controls:

Special, unique speed controls are being used in Canada. How's this for effective speed control? They install huge fake potholes.

I don't know about you, but that would certainly slow me down! People slow down and actually try to 'straddle' the hole. This is an actual speed control device that is currently in use. It is MUCH cheaper than speed cameras, radar guns, police officers, etc.

Pretty clever - especially when the police move them around every day. Isn't art wonderful? We just use real potholes!

Emergency Call Centre:

An Emergency Call Centre worker has been fired, much to the dismay of her colleagues who are reportedly unhappy about her dismissal.

It seems a male caller dialed the emergency number from a mobile phone stating, 'This is Jonathan Davis and I am very depressed. I'm lying here on a railway track waiting for the train to come so I can finally go to God.'

Apparently, 'Remain calm and stay on the line,' was not considered an appropriate response.'

Home owner:

A man went to the police station wishing to speak with the burglar who had broken into his house the night before.

'You'll get your chance in court,' the sergeant said.

'No, no, no!' said the man. 'I want to know how he got into the house without waking my wife. I've been trying to do that for years!'

Bank robber:

A bank robber wanted to keep his identity secret, but didn't wear a balaclava. He told all in the bank not to look at him or he would shoot them. One foolhardy customer sneaked a look and the robber promptly shot him.

The robber asked if anyone else had seen his face.

One customer, gazing intently at the ground, said, 'I think my wife got a glimpse of you.'

The zoo:

A boy with a monkey on his shoulder was walking down the road when he passed a policeman who said, 'Now, now young lad. I think you had better take that monkey to the zoo.'

The next day, the boy was walking down the road with the monkey on his shoulder again, when he passed the same policeman.

The policeman said, 'Hey there. I thought I told you to take that monkey to the zoo!'

The boy answered, 'I did. Today, I'm taking him to the movies.'

Off with his head:

A count who was the leader of a rebel movement was thrown into prison. The king confronted him and demanded to know the names of the other rebels, but he refused.

'Behead him!' the king orders and the count is dragged to the place of execution.

'If you tell me the names I want, I will spare you,' the king said, but still the count refuses to talk.

As the count's head is positioned under the blade, the king warns, 'This is your last chance!'

But the count remains silent.

'Go ahead,' the king orders and the executioner makes his move.

At that moment, the count's nerve broke, 'Wait! Wait! I'll tell you.'

But it was too late The axe had done its work. Furious, the king turned to the executioner. 'How often have I told you,' he yelled, 'not to hatchet your counts before they chicken?'

Golf Club Murder:

Police are called to an apartment and find a woman holding a bloody three-iron, standing over a lifeless man. The detective asks, 'Ma'am, is that your husband?'

'Yes,' replies the woman.

'Did you it him with that golf club?'

'Yes, yes, I did.' The woman begins to sob, drops the club and puts her hands on her face.'

'How many times did you hit him?'

'I don't know – put me down for a five.'

CHAPTER 7

TRAVEL

Scared of flying

An air traffic control tower suddenly lost communication with a small twin engine aircraft. A moment later the tower land line rang and was answered by one of the employees.

The passenger riding with the pilot who lost communications was on a cellular phone and yelled, 'Mayday, mayday!! The pilot had an instant and fatal heart attack. I grabbed his cell phone out of his pocket and he had told me before we took off he had the tower on his speed dial memory. I'm flying upside down at 18,000 feet and traveling at 180 mph. Mayday, mayday!!'

The employee in the tower had put him on speaker phone immediately.

'Calm down, we acknowledge you and we'll guide you down after a few questions. The first thing is not to panic, remain calm!!'

He began his series of questions:

Tower: 'How do you know you are traveling at 18,000 feet?'

Aircraft: 'I can see that it reads 18,000 feet on the Altimeter Dial in front of me.'

Tower: 'Okay, that's good, remain calm. How do you know you're traveling at 180 mph?'

Aircraft: 'I can see that it reads 180 mph on the Airspeed dial in front of me.'

Tower: 'Okay, this is great so far, but it's heavily overcast, so how do you know you're flying upside down?'

Aircraft: 'The sh*t in my pants is running out of my shirt collar.'

Airplane Food - True Story:

Airborne approximately thirty minutes on an outbound evening flight from Glasgow, the lead flight attendant for the cabin crew nervously made the following painful announcement: 'Ladies and gentlemen, I'm so very sorry but it appears that there has been a terrible mix-up one minute prior to take-off, by our airport catering service. I don't know how this has happened but we have 103 passengers on board and, unfortunately, only 40 dinner meals. I truly apologise for this mistake and inconvenience.'

When passengers' muttering had died down, she continued, 'Anyone who is kind enough to give up their meal so that someone else can eat will receive free, unlimited drinks for the duration of our five-hour flight.'

Her next announcement came 90 minutes later. 'If anyone would like to change their minds, we still have 40 dinners available.'

Cruise Ship Complaints:

1. A couple claimed the captain was 'rude' because he did not wait two hours for them at a port, even though they had left him a note earlier that they had 'too much to do.'
2. A man on a cruise around Alaska requested compensation for the warmer clothes he had to buy after failing to 'get an impressive tan' and being unable to 'swim in the swimming pool every day.'
3. A couple said the service was so excellent on a cruise that they spent a lot more on tips than they expected and wanted their gratuities to be refunded.
4. A husband on a two-week honeymoon cruise complained that the staff did not decorate the cab in white, did not scatter rose petals everywhere each morning and did not deliver champagne and strawberries via a private butler. The man requested

special service; he just expected the cruise staff to 'know.'
5. A young woman had heard that British singer Gary Barlow once took the same cruise, so she demanded to know why he wasn't on the same cruise again when she booked it.
6. 'It took us nine hours to fly home from Jamaica to England. It only took the Americans three hours to get home.'
7. 'My fiancé and I booked a twin-bedded cabin but were placed in a double-bedded cabin. We now hold you responsible for the fact that I find myself pregnant. This would not have happened if you had put us in the room that we had booked.'
8. The brochure stated: 'No hairdressers on the ship. We're trainee hairdressers – will we be okay?'
9. 'We had to queue outside to catch the boat and there was no air conditioning.'
10. A woman threatened to call the police after claiming that she had been locked in by staff, when in fact, she had mistaken the 'do not disturb' sign on the back of the door as a warning to remain in the room.
11. One fashion-conscious cruiser was heard complaining to staff during a safety drill that her orange life jacket didn't match her shoes.
12. One disgruntled guest complained that the ship's photographer had deliberately made her 'look ugly' in the photos he took of her.
13. A couple expressed disappointment that their ship didn't look like the Titanic and that its dissimilarity to the doomed ship should have been made clear.
14. A man once asked the captain to turn the engine off because it was too loud.
15. A first-time cruise passenger blamed the captain for not warning him that he could get seasick and asked for a schedule of cruises he could take where he wouldn't get seasick.

16. A man complained, 'On my holiday to Goa in India, I was disgusted to find that almost every restaurant served curry. I don't like spicy food at all!'

Complaints received by travel agents:

1. 'I think it should be explained in the brochure that the local convenience store does not sell proper biscuits like custard creams or ginger nuts.'
2. 'We found the sand was not the sand in the brochure. The brochure shows the sand as being yellow, but it was white.'
3. 'The beach was too sandy. We had to clean everything when we returned to our room.'
4. 'Topless sunbathing on the beach should be banned. The holiday was ruined because my husband spent all day looking at other women.'
5. 'It's lazy of the local shopkeepers to close in the afternoons. I needed to buy things during the *siesta* time – this should be banned.'
6. 'I was bitten by a mosquito – no one said they could bite.'
7. 'We booked an excursion to a water park, but no one told us we had to bring our own bathing suits and towels. We assumed it would be included in the price.'
8. 'No one told us there would be fish in the sea. The children were startled.'
9. 'Although the brochure said that there was a fully equipped kitchen, there was no egg-slicer in the drawers.'
10. 'We went on a holiday to Spain and had a problem with the taxi drivers because they were all Spanish.'
11. 'When we were in Spain, there were too many Spanish people there. The receptionist spoke Spanish; the food was Spanish. No one told us that there would be so many foreigners.'
12. 'It's your duty as a tour operator to advise us of noisy or unruly guests before we travel.'

Smart answer 4

It was mealtime during a flight on a Qantas plane: 'Would you like dinner?' the flight attendant asked one passenger.
'What are my choices?' the man asked.
'Yes or no,' she replied.

Smart answer 3: A lady was picking through the frozen chickens at a Countdown store but she couldn't find one big enough for her family. She asked a passing assistant, 'Do these chickens get any bigger?'

The assistant replied, 'I'm afraid not madam, they're dead.'

Smart answer 2: The policeman flagged down a speeding car and when it stopped, he saw that the driver was a teenager.

'I've been waiting for you all day,' the cop said.

The kid replied, 'Well I got here as fast as I could.'

When the policeman finally stopped laughing, he sent the kid on his way without a ticket.

Smart answer 1: A truck driver was driving along on a country road. A sign came up that read, 'Low Bridge Ahead'. Before he realised it, the bridge was directly ahead and he got stuck under it. Cars were backed up for miles.

Finally, a police car arrived. The policeman got out of his car and walked to the truck's cab and said to the driver, 'Got stuck, eh?'

The truck driver said, 'No, I was delivering this bridge and ran out of fuel!'

Stormy night:

It was a dark and stormy night (of course) off the Wairarapa Coast a hundred years ago and two flashing lights were ominously coming closer and closer, each signalling in Morse Code as radio contact had been lost from lightning static.

The first flashing light messaged: 'Please change your direction 15 degrees to north to avoid a collision.'

The second flashing light responded: 'Highly recommend you divert your course 15 degrees to south to avoid a collision.'

First flashing light: 'This is the captain of an English passenger liner. I say again, divert your course.'

The second flashing light came back with: 'No. I say again, you divert your course.'

First flashing light: 'This is Captain Duncan from the White Star Line and I am in charge of Britain's largest and proudest ocean liner with 1,200 passengers on board and I command that you divert your course now or face the consequences.'

Second flashing light: 'This is Jack, the lighthouse keeper at Castlepoint lighthouse. Your call.'

Air Force Pilot:

During a commercial airline flight, an experienced air force pilot was seated next to a young mother with a baby in her arms. When the baby began crying during the descent for landing, the mother started nursing the infant as discreetly as possible.

The pilot pretended not to notice and upon disembarking, he gallantly offered his assistance to help with the various baby-related items.

When the young mother expressed her gratitude, the pilot responded, 'That's a good-looking baby, and he sure was hungry!'

Somewhat embarrassed, the mother explained that her paediatrician said time spent on the breast would help alleviate the pressure in the baby's ears.'

The air force pilot sadly shook his head and exclaimed, 'And all these years I've been chewing gum.'

Chinese Brochure: (true)

Getting there: A representative will make you wait at the airport. The hotel bus runs along the lake and you will feel pleasure in passing water. You will know the hotel is near, because you will go round the bend. The manager will have intercourse with all new guests.

The Hotel: This is a family hotel, so adultery and children are welcome. Nurses are available in the evenings to put down your children. Guests are invited to conjugate in the bar and expose themselves to others. But please note that ladies are not allowed to have their babies in the bar. We organize social games, so no guest is ever left alone to play with himself.

Your Room: Every room has excellent facilities for your private parts. In winter, every room is on heat. Each room has a balcony offering views of outstanding obscenity. Please feel free to ring for the chambermaid and take advantage of her.

Hospitality: When you leave us at the end of your holiday, l you will struggle to forget it.

With best regards,

The Manager.

CHAPTER 8

CHILDREN

Adam and Eve:

A little girl asked her father, 'How did the human race start?'

The father answered, 'God made Adam and Eve, they had children and so all mankind was made.'

Two days later the girl asked her mother the same question. The mother answered: 'Many years ago there were monkeys from which the human race evolved.'

The confused girl returned to her father and said, 'Dad, how is it possible that you told me the human race was created by God, and Mom said they developed from monkeys?'

The father answered, 'It is very simple. I told you about my side of the family and your mother told you about hers.'

Should Children Witness Childbirth?

Here's your answer.

Due to a power outage, only one paramedic responded to the call. The house was very dark so the paramedic asked Kathleen, a five-year-old girl to hold a flashlight high over her mommy so he could see while he helped deliver the baby.

Very diligently, Kathleen did as she was asked.

Heidi pushed and pushed and after a little while, Connor was born.

The paramedic lifted him by his little feet and spanked him on his bottom. Connor began to cry.

The paramedic then thanked Kathleen for her help and asked the wide-eyed five-year-old what she thought about what she had just witnessed.

Kathleen quickly responded, 'He shouldn't have crawled in there in the first place. Smack his ass again!'

Where babies come from:

- Six-year-old Annie returned home from school and said that today she had her first family planning lesson at school. Her mother, very interested, asks: 'Oh... How did it go?'

    'I nearly died of shame!' she answers. 'Sam from down the street says the stork brings babies. Sally next door said you can buy babies at the orphanage. Pete in my class says you can buy babies at the hospital.'

    Her mother answers laughingly, 'But that's no reason to be ashamed'

    'No... but I can't tell them that we were so poor that you and daddy had to make me yourselves!'

- A child asked his father, 'How were people born?'

    Dad replies, 'Adam and Eve made babies and then their babies became adults and made babies, and so on.'

    The child went to his mother and asked her the same question and his mother replied, 'We were monkeys then we evolved to become like we are now.'

    The peeved child ran back to his dad, 'You lied to me!'

    Dad retorted, 'No, your mother was talking about her side of the family.'

This 'N That

I was driving with my three young children one warm summer evening when a woman in the convertible ahead of us stood up and waved. She was stark naked!

As I was reeling from the shock, I heard my five-year-old shout from the back seat, 'Mom, that lady isn't wearing a seat belt!'

- On the first day of school, a first-grader handed his teacher a note from his mother. It read, 'The opinions expressed by this child are not necessarily those of his parents...'

- A woman was trying hard to get the ketchup out of the bottle. During her struggle the phone rang so she asked her four-year-old daughter to answer the phone. 'Mommy can't come to the phone to talk to you right now, she's hitting the bottle.'

- A little boy got lost at the YWCA and found himself in the women's locker room. When he was spotted, the room burst into shrieks, with ladies grabbing towels and running for cover. The little boy watched in amazement and then asked, 'What's the matter, haven't you ever seen a little boy before?'

- While taking a routine vandalism report at an elementary school, I was interrupted by a little girl about six years old. Looking up and down at my uniform, she asked, 'Are you a cop?'

    'Yes,' I answered and continued writing the report. 'My mother said if I ever needed help I should ask the police. Is that right?''

    'Yes, that's right,' I told her.

    'Well, then,' she said as she extended her foot toward me, 'would you please tie my shoe?'

- It was the end of the day when I parked my police van in front of the station. As I gathered my equipment, my K-9 partner, Jake, was barking, and I saw a little boy staring in at me. 'Is that a dog you got back there?' he asked.

    'It sure is,' I replied.

    Puzzled, the boy looked at me and then towards the back of the van. Finally, he said, 'What did he do?'

- While working for an organization that delivers lunches to elderly shut-ins, I used to take my four-year-old daughter on my afternoon rounds. She was unfailingly intrigued by the various appliances of old age, particularly the canes, walkers and wheelchairs. One day I found her staring at a pair of false teeth soaking in a glass. As I braced myself for the inevitable barrage of questions, she merely turned and whispered, 'The tooth fairy will never believe this!'
- A little girl was watching her parents dress for a party. When she saw her dad donning his tuxedo, she warned, 'Daddy, you shouldn't wear that suit.'

  'And why not, darling?'

  'You know that it always gives you a headache the next morning.'
- A little girl had just finished her first week of school. 'I'm just wasting my time,' she said to her mother. 'I can't read, I can't write, and they won't let me talk!'
- A mother and her young son returned from the grocery store and began putting away the groceries. The boy opened the box of animal crackers and spread them all over the table.

  'What are you doing?' his mother asked.

  'The box says you can't eat them if the seal is broken,' the boy explained. 'I'm looking for the seal.'

Pets are better than children:

Because they:

1. Eat less.
2. Usually come when called.
3. Are easier to train.
4. Don't ask for money all the time.
5. Don't drink or smoke.

6. Don't hang out with friends who use drugs.
7. Never ask to drive the car.
8. Don't have to have the latest fashions.
9. Don't want to wear your clothes.
10. Don't need a gazillion dollars for college, and
11. If they get pregnant, you can sell their children.

When you grow up:

The teacher asks the kids in her third grade class, 'What do you want to be when you grow up?'

Little Jonny says, 'I wanna be a billionaire, go to the most expensive clubs, find me the finest Sheila, give her a Ferrari worth over a million bucks, an apartment in Monte Carlo, a mansion on the beach, a jet to travel all over Europe and an Infinite Visa Card – and have sex with her three times a day.'

He sat down with a big self-satisfied smile. The teacher, shocked and not knowing what to do with this horrible response from little Jonny, decides not to acknowledge what he said and simply tries to continue the lesson and asks, 'And how about you Sandy?'

'Well, I thought I wanted to be a nurse, but now all I want to be is Johnny's Sheila.'

Students aren't stupid!

They walked in tandem, each of the ninety-two students filing into the already-crowded auditorium. With their rich maroon gowns flowing and the traditional caps, they looked almost as grown up as they felt.

Dads swallowed hard behind broad smiles, and Moms freely brushed away tears.

This class would NOT pray during the commencements, not by choice, but because of a recent court ruling prohibiting it 'for fear of offending non-Christians.'

The Principal and several students were careful to stay within the guidelines allowed by the ruling. They gave inspirational and challenging speeches, but no one mentioned divine guidance and no one asked for blessings on the graduates or their families.

The speeches were nice, but they were routine until the final speech received a standing ovation.

A solitary student walked proudly to the microphone. He stood still and silent for just a moment, and then it happened. All 92 students, every single one of them, suddenly SNEEZED in unison!

The student on stage simply looked at the audience and said, 'GOD BLESS YOU,' and then walked off the stage

The audience exploded into applause. This graduating class had found a unique way to invoke God's blessing on their future, with or without the court's approval.

This is a true story; it happened at Eastern Shore District High School in Musquodoboit Harbour, Nova Scotia.

The purchase:

Two young boys walked into a pharmacy one day, picked out a box of tampons and proceeded to the checkout counter. The pharmacist at the counter asked the older boy, 'Son, how old are you?'

'Eight,' the boy replied.

The man continued, 'Do you know what these are used for?'

The boy replied, 'Not exactly, but they aren't for me. They're for him. He's my brother. He's four.'

'Oh, really?' the pharmacist replied with a grin.

'Yes.' the boy said. 'We saw on TV that if you use these, you would be able to swim, play tennis and ride a bike. Right now, he can't do none of that.'

The Outhouse:

Once there was a little boy who lived in the country. For facilities, they had to use an outhouse and the little boy hated it because it was hot in the summer, cold in the winter and stank all the time. The outhouse was sitting on the bank of a creek and the boy decided that one day he would push that outhouse into the water.

One day after a spring rain, the creek was swollen so much that the little boy decided that today was the day to push the outhouse into the creek. So he got a large stick and pushed.

Finally, the outhouse toppled into the creek and floated away.

That night his dad told him they were going to the woodshed after supper. Knowing that meant a spanking, the little boy asked why.

The dad replied, 'Someone pushed the outhouse into the creek today. It was you, wasn't it son?'

The boy answered, 'Yes!' then he thought a moment and said, 'Dad, I read in school today that George Washington chopped down a cherry tree and didn't get into trouble because he told the truth.'

The dad replied, 'Well son, George Washington's father wasn't in that cherry tree!'

Phone Call:

It was Christmas day and a visiting daughter was having lunch with her parents. Half way through the meal, the telephone rang. 'I'll get it,' she said and jumped up to answer it. Her next comment was, 'It's for you Mom,' followed by a loud crash as the phone came away from the wall. The daughter looked incredulously at the phone in her hand and exclaimed, 'My God, it's got a cord!'

Christmas time:

A Sunday school teacher of preschoolers was concerned that his students might be a little confused about Jesus Christ because of the Christmas season's emphasis on His birth. He wanted to make sure they understood that the birth of Jesus occurred a long time ago, that He grew up, etc. So he asked his class, 'Where is Jesus today?'

Steven raised his hand and said, 'He's in heaven.'

Mary was called on and answered, 'He's in my heart.'

Little Johnny, waving his hand furiously, blurted out, 'I know! I know! He's in our bathroom!'

The whole class got very quiet, looked at the teacher and waited for a response. The teacher was completely at a loss for a few very long seconds. He finally gathered his wits and asked Little Johnny how he knew this.

Little Johnny said, 'Well… every morning, my father gets up, bangs on the bathroom door, and yells 'Jesus Crist – are you still in there?'

Lost boy:

My small grandson got lost at the shopping mall. He approached a uniformed security guard and said, 'I've lost my grandpa!'

The guard asked, 'What's his name?'

'Grandpa,' he replied.

The guard smiled then asked, 'What's he like?'

'He likes Crown Royal whiskey and women with big boobs.' Was the innocent reply.

Why teachers continue to drink heavily:

The following questions were in last year's GED examination. (These are genuine answers).

Q. What is a turbine?
A. Something an Arab or Sheik wears on his head. Once an Arab boy reaches puberty, he removes his diaper and wraps it around his head.

Q. How is dew formed?
A. The sun shines down on the leaves and makes them perspire.

Q. What guarantees may a mortgage company insist on?
A. If you are buying a house, they will insist that you are well endowed.

Q. What are steroids?
A. Things for keeping carpets still on the stairs. (Shoot yourself now - there is little hope.)

Q. What happens to your body as you age?
A. When you get old, so do your bowels and you get intercontinental.

Q. What happens to a boy when he reaches puberty?
A. He says goodbye to his boyhood and looks forward to his adultery. (So true.)

Q. Name a major disease associated with cigarettes?
A. Premature death.

Q. How can you delay milk turning sour?
A. Keep it in the cow. (Simple, but brilliant.)

Q. How are the main 20 parts of the body categorized (e.g. The abdomen)?
A. The body is consisted into 3 parts - the brainium, the borax and the abdominal cavity. The brainium contains the brain, the borax contains the heart and lungs and the abdominal cavity contains the five bowels: A,E,I,O,U.

Q. What is the most common form of birth control?
A. Most people prevent contraception by wearing a condominium. (That would work.)

Q. What does the word 'benign' mean?

A. Benign is what you will be after you be eight. (Brilliant.)

Q. Name the four seasons.
A. Salt, pepper, mustard and vinegar.

Storm aftermath:

Ever notice how a four-year-old's voice is louder than 200 adult voices? Several years ago, I returned home from a trip just when a storm hit, with crashing thunder and severe lightning. As I came into my bedroom about 2 a.m., I found my two children in bed with my wife, Karey, apparently scared by the loud storm. I resigned myself to sleep in the guest bedroom that night.

The next day, I talked to the children and explained that it was okay to sleep with Mom when the storm was bad, but when I was expected home, please don't sleep with Mom that night. They said okay.

After my next trip several weeks later, Karey and the children picked me up in the terminal at the appointed time. Since the plane was late, everyone had come into the terminal to wait for my plane's arrival, along with hundreds of other folks waiting for their arriving passengers.

As I entered the waiting area, my son saw me, and came running shouting, 'Hi, Dad! I've got some good news!'

As I waved back, I said loudly, 'What's the good news?'

Alex shouted, 'Nobody slept with Mommy while you were away this time!'

The airport became very quiet, as everyone in the waiting area looked at Alex, then turned to me, and then searched the rest of the area to see if they could figure out exactly who his Mom was.

Choosing a career:

An acquaintance of mine who is a physician told this story about her then four-year-old daughter. On the way to preschool, the doctor had left her stethoscope on the car seat, and her little girl picked it up and began playing with it.

'Be still, my heart,' thought my friend, 'My daughter wants to follow in my footsteps!'

Then the child spoke into the instrument: 'Welcome to McDonald's. May I take your order?'

The allowance:

I was minding my seven-year-old grandson at his house for a week. I asked him if emptying the dishwasher was part of his jobs for pocket money.

He looked up at me in horror and said, 'No way, they only gave me an extra 50c for doing the dishwasher, so I quit. I did start again when they offered me $1 but it still wasn't enough so I quit again and don't do it now.' – A Union Delegate in the making perhaps?

Christmas Mass:

A mother took her three-year-old daughter to Christmas Eve Mass for the first time. The church lights were lowered, and then the choir came down the aisle, carrying lighted candles. All was quiet until the little one started to sing in a loud voice, 'Happy birthday to you…'

Play with boys:

A little girl asked her mother, 'Can I go outside and play with the boys?'

Her mother replied, 'No, you can't play with the boys, they're too rough.'

The little girl thought about it for a few moments and asked, 'If I can find a smooth one, can I play with him?'

Great truths that little children have learned:

1)   No matter how hard you try, you can't baptise cats.

2) When your Mom is mad at your Dad, don't let her brush your hair.
3) If your sister hits you, don't hit her back. They always catch the second person.
4) Never ask your three-year old brother to hold a tomato.
5) You can't trust dogs to watch your food.
6) Don't sneeze when someone is cutting your hair.
7) Never hold a Dust-Buster and a cat at the same time.
8) You can't hide a piece of broccoli in a glass of milk.
9) Don't wear polka-dot underwear under white shorts.
10) The best place to be when you're sad is Grandpa's lap.

Great truths that adults have learned:

1. Raising teenagers is like nailing Jell-O to a tree.
2. Wrinkles don't hurt.
3. Families are like fudge... mostly sweet, with a few nuts.
4. Today's mighty oak is just yesterday's nut that held its ground.
5. Laughing is good exercise. It's like jogging on the inside.
6. Middle-age is when you choose your cereal for the fibre, not the joy.

Great truths about growing old:

1) Growing old is mandatory, growing up is optional.
2) Forget the health food. I need all the preservatives I can get.
3) When you fall down, you wonder what else you can do while you're down there.
4) You're getting old when you get the same sensation from a rocking chair that you once got from a roller coaster.
5) It's frustrating when you know all the answers but nobody bothers to ask you the questions.
6) Time may be a great healer, but it's a lousy beautician.

Money and Addition:

It's a math class and the kids are learning about money and addition.

'If you had $1 and you asked your father for another, how many dollars would you have?' the teacher asked the class.

One child put up his hand and answered, '$1.'

'No,' says the teacher. 'That's incorrect. You don't know how to add up.'

The child quips, 'No, you don't know my father.'

History lesson:

A primary school teacher asked her class during a history lesson, 'When was Rome built?' and one child was first to put up his hand.

'Rome was built at night,' the young boy asked.

'At night?' the teacher replied. 'Whatever gave you that idea?'

'Everyone knows Rome wasn't built in a day,' he replied innocently.

CHAPTER 9

SENIORS

How to call the police when you're old:

George Phillips, an elderly man from Walled Lake, Michigan, was going up to bed, when his wife told him that he'd left the light on in the garden shed, which she could see from the bedroom window. George opened the back door to go turn off the light, but saw that there were people in the shed stealing things. He phoned the police, who asked, 'Is someone in your house?'

He said 'No, but some people are breaking into my garden shed and stealing from me.'

Then the police dispatcher said 'All patrols are busy, you should lock your doors and an officer will be along when one is available.'

George said, 'Okay.'

He hung up the phone and counted to 30 then he phoned the police again.

'Hello, I just called you a few seconds ago because there were people stealing things from my shed. Well, you don't have to worry about them now because I just shot and killed them both; the dogs are eating them right now,' and he hung up.

Within five minutes, six police cars, a SWAT team, a helicopter, two fire trucks, a paramedic and an ambulance showed up at the Phillips' residence and caught the burglars red-handed.

One of the Policemen said to George, 'I thought you said that you'd shot them!'

George said, "I thought you said there was nobody available!'

Lesson learned: Don't mess with old people.

Getting older:

- A distraught senior citizen phoned her doctor's office.

  'Is it true,' she wanted to know, 'that the medication you prescribed has to be taken for the rest of my life?'

  'Yes, I'm afraid so,' the doctor told her.

  There was a moment of silence before the senior lady replied, 'I'm wondering, then, just how serious is my condition because this prescription is marked 'No refills.'

- An older gentleman was on the operating table awaiting surgery and he insisted that his son, a renowned surgeon, perform the operation. As he was about to get the anesthesia, he asked to speak to his son.

  'Yes, Dad, what is it?'

  'Don't be nervous, son; do your best, and just remember, if it doesn't go well, if something happens to me, your mother is going to come and live with you and your wife.'

Senior Prayer:

'Lord, keep Your arm around my shoulder and Your hand over my mouth!'

Aging:

Eventually you will reach a point when you stop lying about your age and start bragging about it. This is so true. I love to hear them say, 'You don't look that old.'

Some people try to turn back their odometers. Not me! I want people to know why I look the way I do. I've travelled a long way and some of the roads weren't paved.

Do you remember being able to get up without making sound effects? Good times... eh?

One of the many things no one tells you about aging is that it is such a nice change from being young.

Be good to your grandkids, one day you'll need them to smuggle grog into your nursing home.

At the root of every grey hair, there is a dead brain cell.

The older we get, the fewer things seem worth waiting for in line. (Mostly because we forgot why we were waiting in line in the first place.)

When you're dissatisfied and would like to go back to youth, think of algebra.

Life begins at 50 – but so does arthritis and the habit of telling the same story three times to the same person.

Ah, being young is beautiful, but being old is comfortable.

First you forget names, then you forget faces, then you forget to pull up your zipper – and it's worse when you forget to pull it down.

Frustration is trying to find your glasses without your glasses.

As I grow older, my mind doesn't just wander – sometimes it buggers off completely.

Old age is coming at a really bad time!

Blessed are those who can give without remembering and take without forgetting.

The irony of life is that, by the time you're old enough to know your way around, you're not going anywhere.

I was always taught to respect my elders, but it keeps getting harder to find one.

Be the reason someone smiles today – or the reason they drink – whatever works for you.

Every morning is the dawn of a new error.

Aspire to inspire before you expire.

Do not regret growing older. It is a privilege denied to many.

'I'm going to retire and live off my savings. Not sure what I'll do that second week.'

It's sad, but as I get older – I think differently!

After a long day on the golf course, I stopped in at Hooter's to see some friends and have some hot wings and iced tea. After being there for a while, one of my friends asked me which waitress I would like to be stuck in an elevator with.

I told them 'The one who knows how to fix elevators.'

You see, I'm old, I'm tired and I pee a lot.

God's plan for aging:

Today is the oldest you've ever been, yet the youngest you'll ever be, so enjoy this day while it lasts.

Most seniors never get enough exercise. In His wisdom, God decreed that seniors become forgetful so they would have to search for their glasses, keys and other things thus doing more walking. And God looked down and saw that it was good.

Then God saw there was another need. In His wisdom, He made seniors lose coordination so they would drop things requiring them to bend, reach and stretch. And God looked down and saw that it was good.

Then God considered the function of bladders and decided seniors would have additional calls of nature requiring more trips to the bathroom, thus providing more exercise. God looked down and saw that it was good.

So if you find as you age, you are getting up and down more, remember it's God's will. It's all in your best interest even though you mutter under your breath.

Nine important facts to remember as we grow older:

#9 Death is the number 1 killer in the world.

#8 Life is sexually transmitted.

#7 Good health is merely the slowest possible rate at which one can die.

#6 Men have 2 motivations: hunger and hanky-panky, and they can't tell them apart. If you see a gleam in his eyes, make him a sandwich.

#5 Give a person a fish and you feed them for a day. Teach a person to use the Internet and they won't bother you for weeks, months, maybe years.

#4 Health nuts are going to feel stupid someday, lying in the hospital, dying of nothing.

#3 All of us could take a lesson from the weather. It pays no attention to criticism.

#2 In the 60's, people took acid to make the world weird. Now the world is weird, and people take Prozac to make it normal.

#1 Life is like a jar of jalapeno peppers. What you do today may be a burning issue tomorrow.

Don't ignore this message. This is your only warning.

How old are you?

Do you realise that the only time in our lives when we like to get old is when we're kids? If you're less than 10 years old, you're so excited about ageing that you think in fractions.

'How old are you?'

'I'm four and a half!'

You're never thirty-six and a half. You're four and a half, going on five! That's the key.

You get into your teens, now they can't hold you back. You jump to the next number, or even a few ahead.

'How old are you?'

'I'm gonna be 16!' You could be 13, but hey, you're gonna be 16 some day!

And then the greatest day of your life: You become 21. YES! Even the words sound like a ceremony.

But then you turn 30. Oooohh, what happened there? Makes you sound like bad milk! S/he 'turned - we had to throw him/her out. There's no fun now, you're Just a sour-dumpling. What's wrong? What's changed?

You become 21, you turn 30, then you're pushing 40... Whoa! Put on the brakes, it's all slipping away. Before you know it, you reach 50 and your dreams are gone.

But wait!!! You make it to 60. You didn't think you would!

You've built up so much speed that you hit 70! After that it's a day-by-day thing.

You get into your 80's and every day is a complete cycle; you hit lunch; you turn 4:30; you reach bedtime. And it doesn't end there. When you're in your 90s, you start going backwards;

'I was just 92.'

Then a strange thing happens. If you make it over 100, you become a little kid again. 'I'm 100 and a half!'

May you all make it to a healthy 100 and a half!!

Senior's Talk:

An elderly gent had been asked to give a talk to his local youth group.

He started by saying, 'I have never taken a strong drink in my life; I have never smoked a cigarette; I have never stayed out of bed after 10:00 pm; have never eaten more than I should; never looked at any woman but my wife and do you know what? Tomorrow, I celebrate my ninety-fifth birthday.'

There was a pause, then a voice from the back asked, 'How do you celebrate? It doesn't sound like you allow yourself to have fun.'

After we go:

A newly retired couple were discussing their future.

'What will you do if I die before you do?' the bloke asks his missus.

After some thought, she said she would probably look for a house-sharing situation with three other single or widowed women who might be a little younger than herself, since she is so active for her age.

Then it was her turn, 'What will you do if I die before you do?'

He replied without a second thought: 'Probably the same thing.'

Random thoughts as we age:

- Wouldn't it be great if we could put ourselves in the dryer for ten minutes; come out wrinkle-free and three sizes smaller!
- Last year I joined a support group for procrastinators. We haven't met yet!
- When I get old, I'm not going to sit around knitting. I'm going to be clicking my life alert button to see how many hot firefighters show up.
- Dear God: My body comes back to you in its original crate – no tattoos, no metal studs, but unfortunately limited in my hearing, sight and possibly body parts missing due to surgery such as tonsils, adenoids, appendix, hysterectomy, prostate surgery, gall bladder, dentures, hearing aids and knee/hip/shoulder replacements.
- I don't trip over things; I do random gravity checks!

- I don't need anger management. I need people to stop pissing me off!
- Old age is coming at a really bad time!
- When I was a child I thought Nap Time was a punishment – now, as a grown up, it just feels like a small vacation!
- The biggest lie I tell myself is –'I don't need to write that down, I'll remember it.'
- 'Lord grant me the strength to accept the things I cannot change, the courage to change the things I can and the friends to post my bail when I finally snap!'
- I don't have grey hair. I have 'wisdom highlights.'
- My people skills are just fine. It's my tolerance to idiots that needs work.
- Teach your daughter how to shoot, because a restraining order is just a piece of paper.
- If God wanted me to touch my toes, he would've put them on my knees.
- The kids text me "plz" which is shorter than please. I text back "no" which is shorter than "yes".
- Even duct tape can't fix stupid, but it can muffle the sound!
- Why do I have to press one for English when you're just gonna transfer me to someone I can't understand anyway?
- Oops! Did I roll my eyes out loud?
- At my age 'Getting lucky' means walking into a room and remembering what I came in there for.
- Chocolate comes from cocoa which is a tree – that makes it a plant which means – chocolate is salad!

- Of course I talk to myself, sometimes I need expert advice.
- Good health is merely the slowest possible rate at which one can die.
- Don't worry about old age; it doesn't last that long.
- Good morning everyone! My body is up - the mind will follow sometime later today.
- Two old men went hunting one day. A hang glider came soaring overhead and the first old man raised his gun and fired. After a brief pause the second old man asked 'Did you get it, whatever it was?'

    The first old man replied 'No, I think I missed it. But I sure as heck made it turn loose that poor fella it was carrying away!'

Now that I'm older, here's what I've discovered:

1. I started out with nothing, and I still have most of it.
2. My wild oats are mostly enjoyed with prunes and all-bran.
3. Funny, I don't remember being absent-minded.
4. Funny, I don't remember being absent-minded.
5. If all is not lost, then where the heck is it?
6. It was a whole lot easier to get older than it was to get wiser.
7. Some days, you're the top dog, some days you're the hydrant.
8. I wish the buck really did stop here, I sure could use a few of them.
9. Kids in the back seat cause accidents. Accidents in the back seat cause kids.
10. It is hard to make a comeback when you haven't been anywhere.

11. My people skills are just fine. It's my tolerance to idiots that needs work.
12. The world only beats a path to your door when you're in the bathroom.
13. When I'm finally holding all the right cards, everyone wants to play chess.
14. It is not hard to meet expenses. They're everywhere.
16. The only difference between a rut and a grave is the depth.
17. These days, I spend a lot of time thinking about the hereafter. I go somewhere to get something and then wonder what I'm 'here after.'
18. Funny, I don't remember being absent-minded.
19. It is a lot better to be seen than viewed.
20. Inside every older person is a younger person wondering, 'What the Hell happened!'
21. Have I sent this message to you before... or did I get it from you?

Thought for the day

There is more money being spent on breast implants and Viagra today than on Alzheimer's research. This means that by 2025, there should be a large elderly population with perky boobs, huge erections and absolutely no recollection of what to do with them.

I am a Seenager: (Senior teenager)

- I have everything I wanted as a teenager, only 60 years later.
- I don't have to go to school or work.
- I get an allowance every fortnight.
- I have my own pad.
- I don't have a curfew.

- I have a driver's license and my own car.
- I have ID that gets me into bars and the liquor shop.
- The people I hang around with are not scared of getting pregnant.
- And I don't have acne.
- Life is great!

Also, you will feel more intelligent after reading this.

- Brains of older people are slow because they know so much.
- People do not decline mentally with age, it just takes them longer to recall facts because they have more information in their brains, scientists believe.
- Much like a computer struggles as the hard drive gets full, so too do humans, and take longer to access information when their brains are full.
- Researchers say this slowing down process is not the same as cognitive decline.
- 'The human brain works slower in old age,' said Dr. Michael Ramscar, 'but only because we have stored more information over time. The brains of older people do not get weak. On the contrary, they simply know more.'
- Also, older people often go to another room to get something and when they get there, they stand there wondering what they came for. It is NOT a memory problem, it's nature's way of making older people do more exercise. SO THERE!

The Umbrella and when to open it:

This actually happened in an Underground station in London. There were protesters on the station concourse handing out pamphlets on the evils of the UK. I politely declined to take one. An elderly woman behind me was getting off the escalator and a young (twentyish) female protester offered her a pamphlet, which she politely declined.

The young protester put her hand on the woman's shoulder as a gesture of friendship and in a very soft voice said, 'Madam, don't you care about the children of Iraq?'

The elderly woman looked up at her and said, 'My dear, my father died in France during World War 2, I lost my husband in Korea and my grandson in Afghanistan. All three died so you could have the right to stand here and bad-mouth our Country. If you touch me again, I'll stick this umbrella up your ass and trust me, I'll open it!'

Don't you just love this lady!

Strip:

When I was at the checkout and ready to pay for my groceries the cashier said, 'strip down, facing me.'

Making a mental note so I could complain to my local MP about this security rubbish, I did just as she had instructed. After the shrieking and hysterical remarks finally subsided, I found that she was referring to how I should position my bank card.

Nevertheless, I've been asked to shop elsewhere in the future. They need to make their instructions a little clearer for seniors. I hate this getting older stuff.

Doesn't need glasses:

My grandfather is eighty and still doesn't need glasses - he drinks straight out of the bottle.

CHAPTER 10

BLONDE JOKES

What's the world coming to?

(1) Recently, I went to McDonald's and I saw on the menu that you could have an order of 6, 9 or 12 Chicken McNuggets. I asked for a half dozen nuggets.

'We don't have half dozen nuggets,' said the teenager at the counter.

'You don't?' I replied.

'We only have six, nine, or twelve,' was the reply.

'So I can't order a half dozen nuggets, but I can order six?'

'That's right.'

So I shook my head and ordered six McNuggets.

(Unbelievable but sadly true... Must have been the same one I asked for sweetener and she said they didn't have any, only Splenda and sugar. And they think they're worth $15.00 per hour?)

(2) I was checking out at the local Wal-Mart with just a few items and the lady behind me put her things on the belt close to mine. I picked up one of those dividers that they keep by the cash register and placed it between our things so they wouldn't get mixed. After the girl had scanned all of my items, she picked up the divider, looking it all over for the bar code so she could scan it.

Not finding the bar code, she said to me, 'Do you know how much this is?'

I said to her 'I've changed my mind; I don't think I'll buy that today.'

She said, 'Okay,' and I paid her for the things and left.

She had no clue to what had just happened. (But the lady behind me had a big smirk on her face as I left.)

(3) A woman at work was seen putting a credit card into her DVD drive and pulling it out very quickly.

When I inquired as to what she was doing, she said she was shopping on the Internet and they kept asking for a credit card number, so she was using the ATM thingy. (Keep shuddering!)

(4) I recently saw a distraught young lady weeping beside her car.

'Do you need some help?' I asked.

She replied, 'I knew I should have replaced the battery to this remote door un-locker. Now I can't get into my car. Do you think they (pointing to a distant convenience store) would have a battery to fit this?'

'Hmm, I don't know. Do you have an alarm, too?' I asked.

'No, just this remote thingy,' she answered, handing it and the car keys to me.

As I took the key and manually unlocked the door, I replied, 'Why don't you drive over there and check about the batteries. It's a long walk...'

(5) Several years ago, we had an Intern who was none too swift. One day she was typing and turned to a secretary and said, 'I'm almost out of typing paper. What do I do?'

'Just use paper from the photocopier,' the secretary told her. With that, the intern took her last remaining blank piece of paper, put it on the photocopier and proceeded to make five blank copies. (A brunette, by the way!)

(6) A mother calls 911 very worried asking the dispatcher if she needs to take her kid to the emergency room, the kid had eaten ants. The dispatcher tells her to give the kid some Benadryl and he should be fine, the mother says, 'I just gave him some ant killer...'

Dispatcher: 'Rush him in to emergency right now!'

Life is tough. It's even tougher if you're stupid!

New Darwin awards! *(Some of these are likely blonde!)*

The annual honour is given to the persons who did the gene pool the biggest service by killing themselves in the most extraordinarily stupid way. Last year's winner was the fellow who was killed by a Coke machine which toppled over on top of him as he was attempting to tip a free soda out.

This year's winner was a real rocket scientist! Read on... And remember that each and every one of these is TRUE.

Semi-finalists

#1 A young Canadian man, searching for a way of getting drunk cheaply, because he had no money with which to buy alcohol, mixed gasoline with milk. Not surprisingly, this concoction made him ill, and he vomited into the fireplace in his house. The resulting explosion and fire burned his house down, killing both him and his sister.

#2 Three Brazilian men were flying in a light aircraft at low altitude when another plane approached. It appears that they decided to moon the occupants of the other plane, but lost control of their own aircraft and crashed. They were all found dead in the wreckage with their pants around their ankles.

#3 A 22-year-old Reston, VA, man was found dead after he tried to use octopus straps to bungee jump off a 70-foot railroad trestle. Fairfax County police said Eric Barcia, a fast food worker, taped a bunch of these straps together, wrapped an end around one foot, anchored the other end to the trestle at Lake Accotink Park, jumped and hit the pavement. Warren Carmichael, a police spokesman, said investigators think Barcia was alone because his car was found nearby. The length of the cord that he had assembled was greater than the distance between the trestle and the ground,' Carmichael said. Police say the apparent cause of death was 'Major trauma.'

#4 A man in Alabama died from rattlesnake bites. It seems that he and a friend were playing a game of catch, using the rattlesnake as a ball. The friend - no doubt a future Darwin Awards candidate - was hospitalized.

#5 Employees in a medium-sized warehouse in west Texas noticed the smell of a gas leak. Sensibly, management evacuated the building extinguishing all potential sources of ignition; lights, power, etc. After the building had been evacuated, two technicians from the gas company were dispatched. Upon entering the building, they found they had difficulty navigating in the dark. To their frustration, none of the lights worked.

Witnesses later described the sight of one of the technicians reaching into his pocket and retrieving an object that resembled a cigarette lighter! Upon operation of the lighter-like object, the gas in the warehouse exploded, sending pieces of it up to three miles away. Nothing was found of the technicians, but the lighter was virtually untouched by the explosion. The technician suspected of causing the blast had never been thought of as "bright' by his peers.

Winner of Darwin Award: (awarded, as always, posthumously.)

The Arizona Highway Patrol came upon a pile of smouldering metal embedded in the side of a cliff rising above the road at the apex of a curve. The wreckage resembled the site of an airplane crash, but it was a car. The type of car was unidentifiable at the scene. Police investigators finally pieced together the mystery.

An amateur rocket scientist had somehow gotten hold of a J A T O unit (Jet Assisted Take Off - actually a solid-fuel rocket) that is used to give heavy military transport planes an extra 'push' for taking off from short airfields. He had driven his Chevy Impala out into the desert and found a long, straight stretch of road.

He attached the J A T O unit to the car, jumped in, got up some speed and fired off the J A T O!

The facts as best as could be determined are that the operator of the 1967 Impala hit the J A T O ignition at a distance of approximately 3.0 miles from the crash site. This was established by the scorched and melted asphalt at that location.

The J A T O, if operating properly, would have reached maximum thrust within 5 seconds, causing the Chevy to reach speeds well in excess of 350 mph and continuing at full power for an additional 20 -25 seconds. The driver, and soon to be pilot, would have experienced G-forces usually reserved for dog fighting F -14 jocks under full afterburners, causing him to become irrelevant for the remainder of the event.

However, the automobile remained on the straight highway for about 2.5 miles (15-20 seconds) before the driver applied and completely melted the brakes, blowing the tires and leaving thick rubber marks on the road surface, then becoming airborne for an additional 1.4 miles and impacting the cliff face at a height of 125 feet leaving a blackened crater three feet deep in the rock. Most of the driver's remains were not recoverable.

However, small fragments of bone, teeth and hair were extracted from the crater, and fingernail and bone shards were removed from a piece of debris believed to be a portion of the steering wheel.

Epilogue: It has been calculated that this moron attained a ground speed of approximately 420-mph, though much of his voyage was not actually on the ground. You couldn't make this stuff up, could you?

And these people are all around us, breeding and voting!

The Heart Attack:

A blonde gets home from work early and hears strange noises coming from the bedroom. She rushes upstairs only to find her husband naked lying on the bed, sweating and panting.

'What's up?' she asks.

'I think I'm having a heart attack,' cries the husband.

The blonde rushes downstairs to grab the phone, but just as she's dialling, her four-year-old son comes up and says, 'Mommy, Mommy, Auntie Shirley is hiding in the wardrobe and she has no clothes on.'

The blonde slams the phone down and storms back upstairs into the bedroom right past her husband, rips open the wardrobe door and sure enough, there is her sister, totally naked and cowering on the floor.

'You rotten bitch!' she screams, 'My husband's having a heart attack, and you're running around naked, and playing hide and seek with the kids.'

Wedding anniversary:

A young man wanted to get his beautiful blonde wife something nice for their first wedding anniversary. So he bought her a cell phone. He showed her the phone and explained to her all of its features.

She was excited to receive the gift and simply adored her - new phone. The next day she went shopping. Her phone rang, and to her astonishment, it was her husband on the other end.

'Hi Darling,' he said, 'How do you like your new phone?'

She replied, 'I just love it! It's so small and your voice is as clear as a bell, but there's one thing I don't understand though,'

'What's that sweetie?' asked her husband.

She replied, 'How did you know I was at Bunnings?'

CHAPTER 11

RELIGIOUS JOKES

A senior church moment:

A Preacher was explaining that he must move on to a larger congregation that will pay him more. There is a hush within the congregation. No one wanted him to leave. Joe Smith, who owns several car dealerships in the city stands up and proclaims, 'If the Preacher stays, I will provide him with a new Cadillac every year, and his wife with a Honda mini-van to transport their children!'

The congregation sighs in relief, and applauds. And another member says, 'If the Preacher will stay on here, I'll personally double his salary, and also establish a foundation to guarantee the college education of all his children!' More sighs and loud applause.

Sadie Jones, age 88, stands and announces with a smile, 'If the Preacher stays, I will give him sex!'

There is total silence. The Preacher, blushing, asks her, 'Mrs. Jones, whatever possessed you to say that?'

Sadie's 90-year-old husband Jake is now trying to hide, holding his forehead with the palm of his hand, and shaking his head from side to side, while his wife replies, 'Well, I just asked my husband how we could help, and he said 'Screw him!'

Isn't senility great? Lord, keep your arm around my shoulder and your hand over my mouth when I get old.

The rain:

- A man goes into the confession booth at the church. 'Forgive me father, for I have sinned.'

    'What is your sin, my son?' Asks the priest.

'Well, about a month ago I was in the library until closing time, and when I wanted to leave it started to rain very heavily and didn't let up. After some time me and the librarian lost our patience and... well... partied all night, if you catch my drift.'

'That is bad but not horrible, my son,' said the priest, 'if it is a one-time slip, God will forgive you.'

'That's just the thing,' said the man, 'about a week ago I helped my neighbor fix her shutters, and when I wanted to go home it started raining heavily and... well... you know, all night long.'

The priest remains silent. The man covers his face in his hands and starts sobbing, 'What should I do now, father?'

'What should you do? screamed the priest, 'You should get out of here right now before it rains!'

- A little boy opened the big family Bible. He was fascinated as he fingered through the old pages. Suddenly, something fell out of the Bible. He picked up the object and looked at it. What he saw was an old leaf that had been pressed in between the pages.

  'Mama, look what I found,' the boy called out.

  'What have you got there, dear?'

  With astonishment in the young boy's voice, he answered, 'I think it's Adam's underwear!'

- While walking along the sidewalk in front of his church, our minister heard the intoning of a prayer that nearly made his collar wilt. Apparently, his five-year-old son and his playmates had found a dead robin. Feeling that a proper burial should be performed, they had secured a small box and cotton batting, then dug a hole and made ready for the disposal of the deceased. The minister's son was chosen to say the appropriate prayers and with sonorous dignity intoned his version of what he thought his father always said: 'Glory be unto the Father, and unto the Son, and into the hole he goes.'

(I want this line used at my funeral!)

The Sermon:

Pope Francis recently finished his sermon.

He ended it with the Latin phrase, "Tuti Homini" - Blessed be Mankind…

A Woman's Rights Group approached the Pope the next day. They noticed that the Pope blessed all Mankind, but not Womankind. So the next day, after his sermon, the Pope concluded by saying, 'Tuti Homini, et Tuti Femini' – 'Blessed be Mankind and Womankind.'

The day after, a Gay Rights Group approached the Pope. They said that they noticed that he blessed Mankind and Womankind and asked if he could also bless gay people.

The Pope said, 'Sure.'

The next day the Pope concluded his sermon with, 'Tuti Homini, et Tuti Femini, et Tuti Fruiti.'

How Moses got the 10 commandments:

God went to the Arabs and said, 'I have Commandments for you that will make your lives better.'

The Arabs asked, 'What are Commandments?'

And the Lord said, 'They are rules for living.'

'Can you give us an example?'

'Thou shall not kill.'

'Not kill? We're not interested.'

So He went to the Blacks and said, 'I have Commandments.'

The Blacks wanted an example, and the Lord said, 'Honour thy Father and Mother.'

'Father? We don't know who our fathers are. We're not interested.'

Then He went to the Mexicans and said, 'I have Commandments.'

The Mexicans also wanted an example, and the Lord said 'Thou shall not steal.'

'Not steal? We're not interested.'

Then He went to the French and said, 'I have Commandments.'

The French too wanted an example and the Lord said, 'Thou shall not commit adultery.'

'Sacre bleu!!! Not commit adultery? We're not interested.'

Finally, He went to the Jews and said, 'I have Commandments.'

'Commandments?' They said, 'How much are they?'

'They're free.'

'We'll take 10.'

There. That, should piss off just about everybody.

Baptism:

An Irishman is stumbling through the woods, totally drunk, when he comes upon a preacher baptizing people in the river. He proceeds into the water, subsequently bumping into the preacher.

The preacher turns around and is almost overcome by the smell of alcohol, whereupon he asks the drunk, 'Are you ready to find Jesus?'

The drunk shouts, 'Yes, I am.'

So the preacher grabs him and dunks him in the water. He pulls him back and asks, 'Brother, have you found Jesus?'

The drunk replies, 'No, I haven't found Jesus!

The preacher, shocked at the answer, dunks him again but for a little longer. He again pulls him out of the water and asks, 'Have you found Jesus, brother?'

The drunk answers, 'No, I haven't found Jesus!'

By this time, the preacher is at his wits end and dunks the drunk again - but this time holds him down for about 30 seconds, and when he begins kicking his arms and legs about, he pulls him up.

The preacher again asks the drunk, 'For the love of God, have you found Jesus?'

The drunk staggers upright, wipes his eyes, coughs up a bit of water, catches his breath, and says to the preacher, 'Are you sure this is where he fell in?'

Kids in church:

Three-year-old Reese: 'Our Father, who does art in heaven, Harold is His name. Amen.'

A little boy was overheard praying: 'Lord, if you can't make me a better boy, don't worry about it. I'm having a real good time like I am.'

After the christening of his baby brother in church, Jason sobbed all the way home in the back seat of the car. His father asked him three times what was wrong. Finally, the boy replied, 'That preacher said he wanted us brought up in a Christian home, and I wanted to stay with you guys.'

One particular four-year-old prayed: 'And forgive us our trash baskets as we forgive those who put trash in our baskets.'

A Sunday school teacher asked her children as they were on the way to church service, 'And why is it necessary to be quiet in church?'

One bright little girl replied, 'Because people are sleeping.'

A mother was preparing pancakes for her sons, Evan five, and Ryan three. The boys began to argue over who would get the first pancake. Their mother saw the opportunity for a moral lesson. 'If Jesus were sitting here, He would say, 'Let my brother have the first pancake, I can wait.' Evan turned to his younger brother and said, ' Ryan, you be Jesus!'

A father was at the beach with his children when the four-year-old son ran up to him, grabbed his hand, and led him to the shore where a seagull lay dead in the sand. 'Daddy, what happened to him?' the son asked.

'He died and went to Heaven,' the Dad replied.

The boy thought a moment and then said, 'Did God throw him back down?'

A wife invited some people to dinner. At the table, she turned to their six-year-old daughter and said, 'Would you like to say the blessing?'

'I wouldn't know what to say,' the girl replied.

'Just say what you hear Mommy say,' the wife answered.

The daughter bowed her head and said, 'Lord, why on earth did I invite all these people to dinner?'

Dwarf Nuns:

The seven dwarfs go to the Vatican, and because they are the seven dwarfs, they are immediately ushered in to see the Pope.

Grumpy leads the pack.

'Grumpy, my son,' says the Pope, 'What can I do for you?'

Grumpy asks, 'Excuse me your Excellency, but are there any dwarf nuns in Rome?'

The Pope wrinkles his brow at the odd question, thinks for a moment and answers, 'No, Grumpy, there are no dwarf nuns in Rome '

In the background, a few of the dwarfs start giggling.

Grumpy turns around and glares, silencing them.

Grumpy turns back, 'Your Worship, are there any dwarf nuns in all of Europe?'

The Pope, puzzled now, again thinks for a moment and then answers, 'No, Grumpy, there are no dwarf nuns in Europe.'

'This time, all of the other dwarfs burst into laughter.

Once again, Grumpy turns around and silences them with an angry glare.

Grumpy turns back and says, 'Mr. Pope! Are there ANY dwarf nuns anywhere in the world?'

The Pope, really confused by the questions says, 'I'm sorry, my son, there are no dwarf nuns anywhere in the world.'

The other dwarfs collapse into a heap, rolling and laughing, pounding the floor, tears rolling down their cheeks, as they begin chanting, 'Grumpy shagged a penguin. Grumpy shagged a penguin!'

The Rooster:

The priest in a small Irish village was very fond of the chickens he kept in the hen house out the back of the parish manse. He had a cock rooster and about ten hens.

One Saturday night the cock rooster went missing and as that was the time he suspected cock fights occurred in the village he decided to do something about it at church the next morning.

At Mass, he asked the congregation 'Has anybody got a cock?' - all the men stood up.

'No, No.' he said 'That wasn't what I meant. Has anybody seen a cock?' - all the women stood up.

'No, No.' he said 'That wasn't what I meant. Has anybody seen a cock that doesn't belong to them.' - half the women stood up.

'No, No, he said 'That wasn't what I meant. Has anybody seen my cock?' - all the nuns stood up.

A cool beer:

One hot summer day, two nuns were shopping at a 7-11 store. As they passed the beer cooler, one nun said to the other, 'Wouldn't it be nice to have a nice cold beer or two?'

The second nun replied, 'Indeed it would Sister but I wouldn't feel comfortable buying beer. I'm certain it would cause a scene at the check-out counter.'

'No problem,' said the first nun, 'I can handle that.'

And she picked up a six-pack and headed for the check-out. The cashier had a surprised look on his face when he saw the two nuns with a six-pack of beer.

'We use the beer for washing our hair,' the nun told him. 'At the nunnery we call it Catholic Shampoo.'

Without blinking an eye, the cashier reached under the counter, pulled out a bag of pretzel sticks and placed them in the bag with the six-pack.

Looking the nun straight in the eye, he smiled and said, 'The curlers are on the house.'

The $10,000 telephone Call:

This will give Americans more information about Canada.

A photographer on vacation was inside a church taking photographs when he noticed a golden telephone mounted on the wall with a sign that read '$10,000 per call'.

The American, being intrigued, asked a priest who was strolling by what the telephone was used for.

The priest replied that it was a direct line to heaven and that for $10,000 you could talk to God.

The American thanked the priest and went along his way.

Next stop was in Atlanta. There, at a very large cathedral, he saw the same golden telephone with the same sign under it.

He wondered if this was the same kind of telephone he saw in Orlando and he asked a nearby nun what its purpose was.

She told him that it was a direct line to heaven and that for $10,000 he could talk to God.

'Okay, thank you,' said the American.

He then travelled to Indianapolis, Washington, Boston, Philadelphia, and New York. In every church he saw the same golden telephone with the same '$10,000 per call' sign under it.

The American, upon leaving Vermont decided to travel up to Canada to see if Canadians had the same phone.

He arrived in Canada, and again, in the first church he entered, there was the same golden telephone, but this time the sign under it read '50 cents per call.'

The American was surprised so he asked the priest about the sign. 'Father, I've travelled all over America and I've seen this same golden telephone in many churches. I'm told that it is a direct line to heaven, but in the US the price was $10,000 per call. Why is it so cheap here?'

The priest smiled and answered, 'You're in Canada now, son ... it's a local call.'

Temptations:

A priest and a rabbi were sitting in adjacent seats on an airplane. After a while the priest turned to the rabbi and asked, 'Is it still a requirement of your faith that you not eat pork?'

The rabbi responded, 'Yes, that is still one of our laws.'

The priest then asked, 'Have you ever eaten pork?'

'Yes, on one occasion I did succumb to temptation and ate a bacon sandwich.'

The priest nodded in understanding and went on with his reading. A while later the rabbi spoke up and asked, 'Father, is it still a requirement of your church that you remain celibate?'

The priest replied, 'Yes, that is still very much a part of our faith.'

The rabbi then asked him, 'Father, have you ever fallen to the temptations of the flesh?'

The priest blushingly replied, 'Yes, Rabbi, on one occasion I was weak and broke the pledge of my faith.'

The rabbi nodded understandingly and remained silent for several minutes.

Finally, the rabbi quietly observed, 'Beats the shit out of a bacon sandwich doesn't it?'

Fanny Green:

An Irish man went to confession in St. Patrick's Catholic Church.

'Father,' he confessed, 'it has been one month since my last confession... I had sex with Fanny Green twice last month.'

The priest told the sinner, 'You are forgiven. Go out and say three Hail Mary's.'

Soon thereafter, another Irish man entered the confessional. 'Father, it has been two months since my last confession. I've had sex with Fanny Green twice a week for the past two months.'

This time, the priest questioned, 'Who is this Fanny Green?'

'A new woman in the neighbourhood,' the sinner replied.

'Very well,' sighed the priest. Go and say ten Hail Mary's.

At mass the next morning, as the priest prepared to deliver the sermon, a tall, voluptuous, drop-dead gorgeous red-headed woman entered the sanctuary. The eyes of every man in the church fell upon her as she slowly sashayed up the aisle and sat down right in front of the priest. Her dress was green and very short and she wore matching, shiny emerald-green shoes.

The priest and the altar boy gasped as the woman in the green dress and matching green shoes sat with her legs spread slightly apart, but just enough to realize she wasn't wearing any underwear.

The priest turned to the altar boy and whispered, 'Is that Fanny Green?'

The bug-eyed altar boy couldn't believe his ears but managed to calmly reply, 'No Father, I think it's just a reflection from her shoes'.

Clerical Collar:

A priest was invited to attend a house party. Naturally, he was properly dressed and wearing his priest's collar.

A little boy kept staring at him the entire evening. Finally, the priest asked the little boy what he was staring at. The little boy pointed to the priest's neck.

When the priest finally realized what the boy was pointing at, he asked him, 'Do you know why I am wearing that?'

The boy nodded his head yes, and replied, 'It kills fleas and ticks for up to three months.'

Repent:

A woman had just returned to her home from an evening of church services, when she was startled by an intruder. She caught the man in the act of robbing her home of its valuables and yelled: 'Stop! Acts 2:38! (Repent and be Baptized, in the name of Jesus Christ, so that your sins may be forgiven.)

The burglar stopped in his tracks. The woman calmly called the police and explained what she had done. As the officer cuffed the man to take him in, he asked the burglar: 'Why did you just stand there? All the old lady did was yell a scripture to you.'

'Scripture?' replied the burglar. 'She said she had an axe and two 38's!'

Santa:

Two boys were walking home from Sunday school after hearing a strong sermon about the devil. One said to the other, 'What do you think about all this Satan stuff?'

The other boy replied, 'Well you know how Santa Clause turned out – it's probably just your Dad.'

Just before Christmas, an honest politician, a generous lawyer and Santa Claus were riding in an elevator of a very posh hotel. Just before the doors opened, they all noticed a $20 bill lying on the floor. Which one picked it up? Santa of course, because the other two don't exist.

Car crash:

An elderly couple, having lived a very healthy life - eating well and exercising daily – died tragically in a car crash. At the Pearly Gates, they were met by St. Peter who took them into their mansion which had all the latest gadgets. 'How much is it?' the man asked.

'Nothing,' said "St. Peter. 'This is Heaven, it's all free.'

He then took them to see the championship golf course.

'How much is the membership?' asked the man.

'Nothing,' said St. Peter. 'This is Heaven, it's all free.'

He then took them to the clubhouse for a lavish buffet lunch.

'Where are the low fat options,' asked the man.

'That's the best part,' said St. Peter. 'You can eat as much as you like of whatever you like and you never get fat and you never get sick. This is Heaven.'

The man then flew into a rage and turned to his wife. 'This is all your fault. If it weren't for your blasted bran muffins, I could have been her ten years ago!'

Lost hat:

A man once spent days looking for his new hat. Finally, he decided that he'd go to church on Sunday and sit at the back. During the service he would sneak out and grab a hat from the rack at the front door.

On Sunday, he went to church and sat at the back. The sermon was about the Ten Commandments. He sat through the whole sermon and instead of sneaking out, he waited until the sermon was over and went to talk to the priest.

'Father, I came here today to steal a hat to replace the one I lost. But after your sermon on the Ten Commandments, I changed my mind.'

The priest replied, 'Bless you, my son. Was it when I started to preach, 'Thou shall not steal,' that changed your heart?'

The man responded, 'No, it was the one on adultery. When you started to preach on that, I remembered where I left my hat!'

Holy Humour:

A father was approached by his small son who told him proudly, 'I know what the Bible means!'

His father smiled and replied, 'What do you mean, you 'know' what the Bible means?'

The son replied, 'I do know!'

'Okay,' said his father, 'What does the Bible mean?'

'That's easy, Daddy,' the young boy replied excitedly, 'It stands for 'Basic Information Before Leaving Earth.'

The confessional:

An elderly man walks into a confessional. The following conversation ensues:

Man: 'I'm 92 years old, have a wonderful wife of 70 years, many children, grandchildren and great grandchildren. Yesterday, I picked up two college girls hitch-hiking. We went to a motel, where I had sex with each of them three times.'

Priest, 'Are you sorry for your sins?'

Man, 'What sins?'

Priest, 'What kind of Catholic are you?'

Man, 'I'm Jewish.'

Priest, 'Why are you telling me all this?'

Man, 'I'm 92 years old – I'm telling everybody!'

Meditation:

Buddha was asked, 'What have you gained from meditation?'

He replied, 'Nothing!' then added, 'Let me tell you what I lost: Anger, Anxiety, Depression, Insecurity, Fear of Old Age and Death.'

CHAPTER 12

AT WORK

Money has different names!

- In temple or church, it's called a donation.
- In school, it's a fee.
- In marriage, it's called a dowry.
- In divorce, it's alimony.
- When you owe someone, it's a debt.
- When you pay the government, it's tax.
- In court, it's a fine.
- Civil servant retirees, it's a pension.
- Employer to workers, it's a salary.
- Master to subordinates, it's wages.
- To children, it's an allowance.
- When you borrow from bank, it's a loan.
- When you offer after a good service. it's a tip.
- To kidnappers, it's a ransom.
- Illegally received in the name of service, it's a bribe.

The question is: When a husband gives it to his wife, what do we call it?

Answer: Money given to your wife is called a duty and every man has to do his duty because wives are not duty free.

If money doesn't grow on trees – why do banks have branches?

Common sense is a flower that doesn't grow in everyone's garden.

They had to get a translator in at the benefits office today. Somebody came in speaking English.

Prices subject to change – according to customer's attitude.

Quick thinking:

A man in London walked into the produce section of his local Tesco's supermarket and asked to buy half a head of lettuce. The boy working in that department told him that they only sold whole heads of lettuce. The man was insistent that the boy ask the manager about the matter.

Walking into the back room, the boy said to the manager, 'Some old bastard wants to buy a half a head of lettuce.'

As he finished his sentence, he turned around to find that the man was standing right behind him, so he quickly added, 'and this gentleman kindly offered to buy the other half.'

The manager approved the deal and the man went on his way.

Later, the manager said to the boy, 'I was impressed with the way you got yourself out of that situation earlier, we like people who can think on their feet here, where are you from son?'

'New Zealand, sir,' the boy replied.

'Why did you leave New Zealand?' the manager asked.

The boy said, 'Sir, there's nothing but prostitutes and rugby players there.'

'Is that right?' replied the manager, 'My wife is from New Zealand!'

'Really?' replied the quick-thinking boy. 'Who'd she play for?'

At the checkout:

I was in the six item express lane at the Countdown last night quietly fuming. Completely ignoring the sign, the woman ahead of me had slipped into the check-out line pushing a cart piled high with groceries. Imagine my delight when the cashier beckoned the woman to come forward looked into the cart and asked sweetly, 'So which six items would you like to buy today?'

Wouldn't it be great if that happened more often?

Irish Painter:

The foreman of an Irish road crew employed Paddy to paint the white lines line down the middle of the road. He told Paddy that he should paint two miles of road in a day's work.

After the first day, the foreman was pleased to find that he'd painted four miles of road instead of the two required.

On the second day, Paddy completed painting just two miles of road. The foreman was a bit disappointed, but didn't complain as this was, after all, only what he'd asked for.

On day 3, the foreman was disappointed to find that Paddy had painted only one mile of road, and so asked, 'On yer first day, ya did four moiles of road. On yer second ya did two moiles. But on yer tird day ya only did one moil. What's up?

Paddy replied, 'Well, oil tell ya what's up, but I tought a clever bloke loik you woulda been able ta figger it out fer yerself! Yer see, every day I gets ferder an ferder away from de paint can!'

The best:

Pinocchio, Snow White and Superman are out for a stroll in town one day. As they walk, they come across a sign: 'Beauty contest to find the most beautiful woman in the world.'

'I'm entering that,' said Snow White. After half an hour she comes out and they ask her, 'Well, how'd you do?'

'First Place,' said Snow White.

They continue walking and they see another sign: 'Contest to find the strongest man in the world.'

'I'm entering that,' says Superman. After half an hour he returns and they ask him, 'How did you make out?'

'First Place,' answers Superman. 'Did you ever doubt it?'

They continue walking when they see a sign: 'Contest! Who is the greatest liar in the world?' Pinocchio enters. After half an hour he returns with tears in his eyes. 'What happened?' they asked.

'Who the hell is Hilary Clinton?' asked Pinocchio.

Paddy, The Irish Wrestler

A Russian and an Irish wrestler were set to square off for the Olympic gold medal. Before the final match, the Irish wrestler's trainer came to him and said 'Now, don't forget all the research we've done on this Russian. He's never lost a match because of this 'pretzel' hold he has. It ties you up in knots. Whatever you do, do not let him get you in that hold! If he does, you're finished.'

The Irishman nodded in acknowledgment. As the match started, the Irishman and the Russian circled each other several times, looking for an opening. All of a sudden, the Russian lunged forward, grabbing the Irishman and wrapping him up in the dreaded pretzel hold. A sigh of disappointment arose from the crowd and the trainer buried his face in his hands, for he knew all was lost. He couldn't watch the inevitable happen.

Suddenly, there was a long, high pitched scream, then a cheer from the crowd and the trainer raised his eyes just in time to watch the Russian go flying up in the air. His back hit the mat with a thud and the Irishman collapsed on top of him, making the pin and winning the match.

The trainer was astounded. When he finally got his wrestler alone, he asked 'How did you ever get out of that hold? No one has ever done it before!'

The wrestler answered 'Well, I was ready to give up when he got me in that hold but at the last moment, I opened my eyes and saw this pair of testicles right in front of my face. I had nothing to lose so with my last ounce of strength, I stretched out my neck and bit those babies just as hard as I could.'

The trainer exclaimed 'That's what finished him off?'

'Not really. You'd be amazed how strong you get when you bite your own nuts.'

Text book:

I'd been working on my business degree for about a year when I finally got to take a popular finance course. I went to the bookstore to buy the text and was shocked to find out that it would cost me $96. I asked how much it was worth if I sold it back at the end of the semester.

'You'll get $24,' said the clerk.

'This is insane,' I protested as I wrote out the check.

'I know,' replied the clerk sympathetically. 'I've always thought that a person who buys a finance book for $96 and then sells it back for $24 should fail the course.'

The advantages of not drinking coffee plus being minus.

A guy goes to the Post Office to apply for a job. The interviewer asks him, 'Are you allergic to anything?'

He replies, 'Yes, caffeine. I can't drink coffee.'

'Okay, have you ever been in the military service?'

'Yes,' he says, 'I was in Iraq for one tour.'

The interviewer says, 'That will give you five extra points toward employment'

Then he asks, 'Are you disabled in any way?'

The guy says, 'Yes. A bomb exploded near me and I lost both my testicles.'

The interviewer grimaces and then says, 'Okay. You've got enough points for me to hire you right now. Our normal hours are from 8:00 am to 4:00 pm. You can start tomorrow at 10:00 am, and plan on starting at 10:00 am every day.'

The guy is puzzled and asks, 'If the work hours are from 8:00 am to 4:00 pm, why don't you want me here until 10:00 am?'

'This is a government job,' the interviewer says. 'For the first two hours, we just stand around drinking coffee and scratching our balls. No point in you coming in for that.'

Office memo to all employees

Re: Christmas Party

December 1... To All Employees
I'm happy to inform you that the company Christmas Party will be held on December 23rd at Luigi's Open Pit Barbecue. There will be lots of spiked eggnog and a small band will play traditional carols... feel free to sing along. And don't be surprised if our CEO shows up dressed as Santa Claus to light the Christmas tree. Exchanging gifts among employees can be done at this time. Please remember to keep gifts to the agreed $10 limit. Merry Christmas to you and yours,
Patrick Connolly, Human Resources Director

December 2... To All Employees
In no way was yesterday's memo intended to exclude our Jewish employees. We recognize that Hanukkah is an important holiday and often coincides with Christmas (although not this year). However, from now on we're calling this party our Holiday Party. There will be no tree or Christmas carols sung.
Happy holidays to you and yours.
Patrick Connolly, Human Resources Director

December 3... To All Employees

Regarding the anonymous note I received from a member of Alcoholics Anonymous requesting a non-drinking table, I'm happy to accommodate your request but please remember that if I put a sign on the table that reads 'AA Only' you won't be anonymous any more. In addition, we'll no longer be having a gift exchange because union members feel that $10 is too much money.
Patrick Connolly, Human Resources Director

December 7... To All Employees
I have arranged for members of Overeaters Anonymous to sit farthest away from the dessert table and for pregnant members to sit closest to the restrooms. Gay men are allowed to sit with each other. Lesbians do not have to sit with gays; each group will have its own table. And, yes, there will be a flower arrangement for the gay men's table. Happy now?
Patty Connolly, Human Resources Director

December 9... To All Employees
People! People! Nothing sinister was intended by wanting our CEO to play Santa Claus, even if the anagram for 'Santa' does happen to be 'Satan.' There is no evil connation to our own little 'man in a red suit.'
Patrick Connolly, Human Resources Director

December 10... To All Employees
Vegetarians! I've had it with you people. We're holding this party at Luigi's Open Pit Barbecue whether you like it or not. You can just sit at the table farthest from the 'Grill of Death' as you call it, and you'll get salad bar only, including hydroponic tomatoes. Tomatoes have feelings too, you know. They scream when you slice them. I can hear them now. I hope you all have a rotten holiday.
Patrick Connolly

December 14... To All Employees
I'm sure I speak for all of us in wishing Patrick Connolly a speedy recovery from his stress-related illness. I'll continue to forward your cards to him at the sanitarium. In the

meantime management has decided to cancel the Holiday Party and give everyone the afternoon of the 23rd off with full pay.
Terri Bishop, Acting Human Resources Director

Annual Meeting:

A large corporation was holding its annual meeting of the heads of departments. The chairman turned to the Human Resources Manager and asked: 'How many people do we have employed – broken down by sex?'

The Human Resources Manager thought for a few moments before replying: 'I'm glad to say not too many – excessive drinking is more of a problem for us.'

Starting Salary:

Reaching the end of a job interview, the Human Resources Manager asked a young engineer who was fresh out of university, 'What starting salary were you thinking about?'

The engineer said, 'In the neighbourhood of $125,000 a year, depending on the benefits package.'

The interviewer said, 'Well, what would you say to a package of 5 weeks' vacation, 14 days paid holidays, full medical and dental, company matching retirement fund to 50% of salary, and a company car leased every 2 years – say a red Corvette?'

The engineer sat up straight and said, 'Wow! Are you kidding?'

The interviewer replied, 'Yeah, but you started it.'

Wants a raise:

The boss had listened in sympathetic silence as one of his employees went through the reasons why he needed, and felt he deserved, a raise. Then, with a compassionate smile, the CEO patted the younger man on the shoulder.

'Yes,' he said, 'I know you can't get married on the salary I'm paying you, and some day you'll thank me for it.'

Need a day off:

An office worker makes an appointment to see his supervisor. 'Boss, we're doing some heavy-duty cleaning at home tomorrow and my wife needs me to help clean out the garage and do some work around the yard.' He said.

'We're short-handed,' the boss replied. 'I can't possibly give you the day off.'

'Thanks boss,' the bloke said, 'I knew I could count on you!'

New Soft Drink:

The Pfizer Corporation announced today that Viagra will soon be available in liquid form and this new product will be marketed by Pepsi Cola as a power beverage suitable for use as a mixer.

It will now be possible for a man to literally pour himself a stiff one. Obviously we can no longer call this a soft drink, and it gives new meaning to the names of cocktails, highballs and just a good old-fashioned stiff drink. Pepsi will market the new concoction by the name of: MOUNT & DO.

Different Signs:

- Outside Heaven: 'Lying naked with somebody in bed and screaming Oh God... Oh God.... will not be considered as prayers.'
- Outside a Prayer Hall: 'Please do not leave your bags, wallets, cell phones unattended. Others might think those are the answers to their prayers.'
- Outside a prostitute's house: 'Married men are not allowed. We serve the needy, not the greedy.'
- Outside driving school: 'If your wife wants to learn to drive – don't stand in her way.'

- Outside a library: 'Statutory warning: While reading Kamasutra, please hold the book with both hands.'
- 'Our beer is as cold as your ex's heart.'
- 'Attention: Please be patient with the bartender. Evan a toilet can serve only one asshole at a time.'
- 'Nachos as big as your ass.'
- 'We do not serve women. You must bring your own.'
- 'If you are racist, sexist, homophobic, or an asshole – don't come in.'
- McDonald's: 'Saying your kids are fat because of us – is like saying it's Hooters fault your husband likes big tits.'
- A Psychotherapist had to correct the painter when he mistakenly put the words 'Psycho the Rapist' on the door to his office.
- 'Danger – helicopters operate in this area. If you find yourself walking towards a big noisy thing with spinning blades, turn the f**k around Einstein!'
- 'Danger – do not touch. Not only will this kill you, it will hurt the whole time you are dying.'
- 'Is there life after death? Trespass here and find out.'
- 'Please do not enter the dangerous area beyond this gate! You quite possibly will get hurt, then you will sue, then a protracted court battle will ensue exhausting your financial resources and you will lose because this sign that warned you will be – Exhibit 1.'
- 'Going to jail sale.'
- Instead of a sign that says, 'Do not disturb,' I need one that says 'Already disturbed, proceed with caution.'
- 'I only do what the voices in my wife's head tell her to tell me to do.'
- 'Push – if that doesn't work – pull. If that doesn't work either, that's because we're closed.'
- 'Caution – this machine has no brain – use your own.'
- 'The NAKED truth about our WAITRESSES is they may FLIRT WITH YOU to get a better tip.'

Ethics:

- A father is explaining ethics to his son, who is about to go into business.

  'Suppose a woman comes in and orders $100 worth of material. You wrap it up and you give it to her. She pays you with a $100 note, but as she goes out the door, you realize she's given you two $100 bills.

  Now here's where the ethics come in. Should you or should you not tell your business partner?

- I never wanted to believe that my Dad was stealing from his job as a road worker. But when I got home, all the signs were there.

Faith in your fellow man:

Each one of us is a mixture of good qualities and some perhaps not-so-good qualities. In considering our fellow man, we should remember his good qualities and realize that his faults only prove that he is after all, a human being.

We should refrain from making harsh judgements of a person just because he happens to be a dirty, rotten, no-good son-of-a-bitch!

Anger Management:

My boss asked me to take an anger management course. I told him I'm angry enough with management as it is.'

CHAPTER 13

IS THAT RIGHT?

English is a strange language

Do you know that the words 'listen' and 'silent' use the exact same letters?

Do you also know that the words 'race car' spelled backwards still spells 'race car?'

Do you know that the word 'eat' is the only word where if you take the first letter and move it to the end, it spells its past tense 'ate?'

And have you noticed that if you re-arrange the letters in 'illegal immigrants' and add just a few more letters, they spell: 'Go home you free-loading, benefit-grabbing, resource-sucking, baby-making, non-English-speaking assholes and take those other hairy-faced, sandal-wearing, bomb-making, camel-riding, goat-shagging, raggedy-ass bastards with you?'

How weird is that?

Confucius Say:

- Okay to let a fool kiss you, but not okay to let a kiss fool you.
- Kiss is merely shopping upstairs for real merchandise downstairs.
- Better to lose a lover than love a loser.
- Man with broken condom often called Daddy.
- Drunken man's words often sober man's thoughts.
- Marriage is same as bank account You put it in, you take it out - you lose interest.
- Viagra just like Disneyland. You'll have a one hour wait for two-minute ride.
- Much better to want the mate you do not have, than to have the mate you do not want.

- Joke is just like sex. neither any good if you don't get it.

Did you know?

1. Your shoes are the first thing people subconsciously notice about you. Wear nice shoes.
2. If you sit for more than 11 hours a day, there's a 50% chance you'll die within the next 3 years.
3. There are at least 6 people in the world who look exactly like you. There's a 9% chance that you'll meet one of them in your lifetime.
4. Sleeping without a pillow reduces back pain and keeps your spine stronger.
5. A person's height is determined by his/her father, and his/her weight is determined by the mother.
6. If a part of your body 'falls asleep' you can almost always 'wake it up' by shaking your head. (spooky)
7. There are three things the human brain cannot resist noticing, food, attractive people and danger.
8. Right-handed people tend to chew food on their right side.
9. Right-handed people live, on average, nine years longer than left-handed people do.
10. Putting dry tea bags in gym bags or smelly shoes will absorb the unpleasant odour.
11. According to Albert Einstein, if honey bees were to disappear from earth, humans would be dead within four years.
12. There are so many kinds of apples, that if you ate a new one every day, it would take over twenty years to try all of them.
13. You can survive without eating for weeks, but you will only live eleven days without sleeping.
14. People who laugh a lot are healthier than those who don't. (That's why I write joke books folks.)
15. Laziness and inactivity kills just as many people as smoking.
16. A human brain has the capacity to store five times as much information as Wikipedia. (Wow!)

17. Our brain uses the same amount of power as a 10-watt light bulb! (Sounds as if it isn't very bright!)
18. Our body gives enough heat in 30 minutes to boil 1.5 litres of water. (I must remember this when I forget matches. I do know that my hand is hot enough to 'iron' T-shirts by just rubbing my hands across them.)
19. The ovum egg is the biggest cell and the sperm is the smallest cell! (I told you guys we were better!)
20. Stomach acid (conc. HCL) is strong enough to dissolve razor blades!! (And coca cola is strong enough to dissolve a metal nail and take tar off a car.)
21. Take a 10-30 minute walk every day and while you walk, smile. It's the ultimate anti-depressant.
22. Sit in silence for at least ten minutes each day.
23. Eat more foods that grow on trees and plants and eat less food that is manufactured in plants.
24. Drink green tea and plenty of water. Eat blueberries, broccoli and almonds.
25. Try to make at least three people smile each day.
26. Don't waste your precious energy on gossip, energy vampires, issues of the past, negative thoughts or things you can't control. Instead, invest your energy in the positive present moment.
27. Eat breakfast like a king, lunch like a prince and dinner like a college kid with a maxed-out charge card.
28. Life isn't fair, but it's still good.
29. Life is too short to waste time hating anyone. Forgive them for everything.
30. Don't take yourself so seriously – no one else does.
31. You don't have to win every argument. Agree to disagree occasionally.
32. Make peace with your past so you don't spoil the present.
33. Don't compare your life to others. You have no idea what their journey is all about!
34. No one is in charge of your happiness except you.
35. Frame every so-called disaster with these words: 'In five years will this matter?'

36. Help the needy. Be generous! Be a 'giver' not a 'taker.'
37. What other people think of you is none of your business.
38. Time heals everything.
39. However good or bad the situation is, it will change.
40. Your job won't take care of you when you're sick. Your friends will, so stay in touch.
41. Envy is a waste of time. You already have all you need.
42. Doing what you like is freedom. Liking what you do is happiness.
43. Silence is the best reply to a fool.
44. Remember that you are too blessed to be stressed.
45. If walking is good for your health, the postman would be immortal.
46. A whale swims all day, only eats fish, and drinks water, but is still fat.
47. A rabbit runs and hops and only lives 15 years, while a tortoise doesn't run and does mostly nothing, yet it lives for 150 years. And they tell us to exercise? I don't think so.

More Lexophiles

'Lexophile' is a word used to describe those that have a love for words, such as 'you can tune a piano, but you can't tuna fish,' or 'to write with a broken pencil is pointless.' A competition to see who can come up with the best lexophiles is held every year in an undisclosed location.

This year's winning submission is posted at the very end.

- When fish are in schools, they sometimes take debate.
- A thief who stole a calendar got twelve months.
- When the smog lifts in Los Angeles U.C.L.A.
- The batteries were given out free of charge.
- A dentist and a manicurist married. They fought tooth and nail.
- Police were summoned to a daycare centre where a three-year-old was resisting a rest.

- Did you hear about the fellow whose entire left side was cut off? He's all right now.
- Acupuncture is a jab well done. That's the point of it.

And the cream of the crop:

- Those who get too big for their pants will be totally exposed in the end.

Neologisms:

The Washington Post has published the winning submissions to its yearly neologism contest, in which readers are asked to supply alternative meanings for common words. The winners are:

1. Coffee (n.), the person upon whom one coughs.
2. Flabbergasted (adj.), appalled over how much weight you have gained.
3. Abdicate (v.), to give up all hope of ever having a flat stomach.
4. Esplanade (v.), to attempt an explanation while drunk.
5. Willy-nilly (adj.), impotent.
6. Negligent (adj.), describes a condition in which you absent-mindedly answer the door in your nightgown.
7. Lymph (v.), to walk with a lisp.
8. Gargoyle (n), olive-flavoured mouthwash.
9. Flatulence (n.) emergency vehicle that picks you up after you are run over by a steamroller.
10. Balderdash (n.), a rapidly receding hairline.
11. Testicle (n.), a humorous question on an exam.
12. Rectitude (n.), the formal, dignified bearing adopted by proctologists.
13. Pokemon (n), a Rastafarian proctologist.
14. Oyster (n.), a person who sprinkles his conversation with Yiddish isms.
15. Circumvent (n.), an opening in the front of boxer shorts worn by Jewish men

16. Frisbeetarianism (n.), (back by popular demand): The belief that, when you die, your soul flies up onto the roof and gets stuck there.

Ambiguity:

For those who love the philosophy of ambiguity, as well as the idiosyncrasies of English:

1. If man evolved from monkeys and apes, why do we still have monkeys and apes?
2. The main reason that Santa is so jolly is because he knows where all the bad girls live.
3. Whose cruel idea was it for the word 'lisp' to have 's' in it?
4. Why is there an expiration date on sour cream?
5. If you spin an oriental man in a circle three times, does he become disoriented?
6. Why do shops have signs, 'guide dogs only.' The dogs can't read and their owners are blind?

Albert Einstein Stories

(1) One day during a speaking tour, Albert Einstein's driver, who often sat at the back of the hall during his lectures, remarked that he could probably give the lecture himself, having heard it so many times. So Einstein told the driver that at the next stop on the tour to switch places, with Einstein sitting at the back in the driver's uniform. Having delivered a flawless lecture, the driver was asked a difficult question by a member of the audience. 'Well, the answer to that question is quite simple,' he casually replied. 'I bet my driver, sitting up at the back there, could answer it!'

(2) Albert Einstein's wife often suggested that he dress more professionally when he headed off to work. 'Why should I?' he would invariably argue. 'Everyone knows me there.' When the time came for Einstein to attend his first major conference, she begged him to dress up a bit. 'Why should I?' said Einstein. 'No one knows me there!'

(3) Albert Einstein was often asked to explain the general theory of relativity. 'Put your hand on a hot stove for a minute, and it seems like an hour,' he once declared. 'Sit with a pretty girl for an hour, and it seems like a minute. That's relativity!'

(4) When Albert Einstein was working in Princeton university, one day he was going home, he forgot his home address. The driver of the cab did not recognize him. Einstein asked the driver if he knows Einstein's home. The driver said 'Who does not know Einstein's address? Everyone in Princeton knows. Do you want to meet him?' Einstein replied 'I am Einstein. I forgot my home address, can you take me there?' The driver drove him to his home and did not even collect his fare from him.

(5) Einstein was once traveling from Princeton on a train when the conductor came down the aisle, punching the tickets of every passenger. When he came to Einstein, Einstein reached in his vest pocket. He couldn't find his ticket, so he reached in his trouser pockets. It wasn't there, so he looked in his briefcase but couldn't find it. Then he looked in the seat beside him. He still couldn't find it. The conductor said, 'Dr. Einstein, I know who you are. We all know who you are. I'm sure you bought a ticket. Don't worry about it.' Einstein nodded appreciatively. The conductor continued down the aisle punching tickets. As he was ready to move to the next car, he turned around and saw the great physicist down on his hands and knees looking under his seat for his ticket. The conductor rushed back and said, 'Dr. Einstein, Dr. Einstein, don't worry, I know who you are. No problem. You don't need a ticket. I'm sure you bought one.' Einstein looked at him and said, 'Young man, I too, know who I am. What I don't know is where I'm going.'

(6) With Charlie Chaplin: Einstein said, 'What I admire most about your art, is its universality. You do not say a word, and yet the world understands you.' 'It's true,' replied

Charlie Chaplin, 'but your fame is even greater: The world admires you, when nobody understands you.'

Anagrams:

- Presbyterian: When you re-arrange the letters: Best in prayer
- Astronomer: When you re-arrange the letters: Moon starer
- Desperation: When you re-arrange the letters: The rope ends it
- The eyes: When you re-arrange the letters: They see
- The Morse code: When you re-arrange the letters: Here come the dots
- Dormitory: When you re-arrange the letters: Dirty room
- Slot machines: When you re-arrange the letters: Cash lost in me
- Animosity: When you re-arrange the letters: Is no amity
- Election results: When you re-arrange the letters: Lies – let's recount
- Snooze alarms: When you re-arrange the letters: Alas! No more Z's.
- A decimal point: When you re-arrange the letters: I'm a dot in place
- The earthquakes: When you re-arrange the letters: That queer shake
- Eleven plus two: When you re-arrange the letters: Twelve plus one
- Mother-in-law: When you re-arrange the letters: Woman Hitler

Paraprosdokians

Paraprosdokians are figures of speech in which the latter part of a sentence is unexpected. Winston Churchill loved them.

1. Where there's a will, I want to be in it.
2. The last thing I want to do is hurt you, but it's still on my list.

3. Since light travels faster than sound, some people appear bright until you hear them speak.
4. If I agreed with you, we'd both be wrong.
5. We never really grow up; we only learn how to act in public.
6. War does not determine who is right - only who is left.
7. Knowledge is knowing a tomato is a fruit. Wisdom is not putting it in a fruit salad.
8. They begin the evening news with 'Good Evening,' then proceed to tell you why it isn't.
9. To steal ideas from someone is plagiarism. To steal from many is called research.
10. In filling in an application, where it says, 'In case of emergency, notify:' I put 'DOCTOR.'
11. I didn't say it was your fault, I said I was blaming you.
12. Women will never be equal to men until they can walk down the street with a bald head and a beer gut, and still think they look sexy.
13. Behind every successful man is his woman. Behind the fall of a successful man is usually another woman.
14. You do not need a parachute to skydive. You only need a parachute so you can skydive twice.
15. Money can't buy happiness, but it sure makes misery easier to live with.
16. A clear conscience is the sign of a bad memory.
17. I used to be indecisive. Now I'm not so sure.
18. Nostalgia isn't what it used to be. Nor is there any future in it.
19. Change is inevitable, except from a vending machine.
20. Going to church doesn't make you a Christian any more than standing in your garage makes you a car.
21. I'm supposed to respect my elders, but it's getting harder and harder for me to find one now.

And my personal favourite:

22. I'm not arguing with you; I'm explaining why you are wrong.

Interesting trivia

Glass takes one million years to decompose, which means it never wears out and can be recycled an infinite amount of times!

Gold is the only metal that doesn't rust, even if it's buried in the ground for thousands of years.

Your tongue is the only muscle in your body that is attached at only one end.

If you stop getting thirsty, you need to drink more water. When a human body is dehydrated, its thirst mechanism shuts off.

Zero is the only number that cannot be represented by Roman numerals.

Kites were used in the American Civil War to deliver letters and newspapers.

The song, Auld Lang Syne is sung at the stroke of midnight in almost every English-speaking country in the world to bring in the new year.

Drinking water after eating reduces the acid in your mouth by 61 percent.

Peanut oil is used for cooking in submarines because it doesn't smoke unless it's heated above 450F.

The roar that we hear when we place a seashell next to our ear is not the ocean, but rather the sound of blood surging through the veins in the ear.

Nine out of every 10 living things live in the ocean.

The banana cannot reproduce itself. It can be propagated only by the hand of man.

Airports at higher altitudes require a longer airstrip due to lower air density.

The University of Alaska spans four time zones.

The tooth is the only part of the human body that cannot heal itself.

In ancient Greece tossing an apple to a girl was a traditional proposal of marriage. Catching it meant she accepted.

Warner Communications paid 28 million for the copyright to the song Happy Birthday.

Intelligent people have more zinc and copper in their hair.

A comet's tail always point away from the sun.

The Swine Flu vaccine in 1976 caused more death and illness than the disease it was intended to prevent.

Caffeine increases the power of aspirin and other painkillers, that is why it's found in some medicines.

The military salute is a motion that evolved from medieval times, when knights in armor raised their visors to reveal their identity.

If you get into the bottom of a well or a tall chimney and look up, you can see stars, even in the middle of the day.

When a person dies, hearing is the last sense to go. The first sense lost is sight.

In ancient times strangers shook hands to show that they were unarmed.

Strawberries are the only fruit whose seeds grow on the outside.

Avocados have the highest calories of any fruit at 167 calories per hundred grams.

The moon moves about two inches away from the Earth each year.

The Earth gets 100 tons heavier every day due to falling space dust.

Due to earth's gravity it is impossible for mountains to be higher than 15,000 meters.

Mickey Mouse is known as "Topolino" in Italy.

Soldiers do not march in step when going across bridges because they could set up a vibration which could be sufficient to knock the bridge down.

Everything weighs one percent less at the equator.

For every extra kilogram carried on a space flight, 530 kg of excess fuel are needed at lift-off.

The letter J does not appear anywhere on the periodic table of the elements.

The Canadian

Bob, a middle-aged Canadian tourist on his first time in Lincoln, Nebraska, locates the red light district and enters a large brothel.

The madam asks him to be seated and sends over a young lady to entertain the client. They sit and talk, frolic a little, giggle a bit, drink a bit, and she sits on his lap. He whispers in her ear and she gasps and runs away!

Seeing this, the madam sends over a more experienced lady to entertain the gentleman. They sit and talk, frolic a little, giggle a bit, drink a bit, and she sits on his lap. He whispers in her ear and she screams, 'No!' and walks quickly away!

The madam is surprised that this ordinary looking man has asked for something so outrageous that her two girls will have nothing to do with it. She decides that only her most experienced lady, Lola, will do. Lola looks a bit tired, but she has never said no and it doesn't seem likely that anything would surprise her. So the madam sends her over to Bob.

They sit and talk, frolic a little, giggle a bit, drink a bit, and she sits on his lap. He whispers in her ear and she screams,

'No way Buddy!' smacks him as hard as she can and literally runs away!

Madam is by now absolutely intrigued, having seen nothing like this in all her years of operating a brothel. She hasn't done the bedroom work herself for a long time, but she did it for many years before she got into management. She's sure she has said yes at one time or another to everything a man could possibly ask for. The challenge is irresistible.

She just has to find out what this man has wanted that has made her girls so angry. And she sees a chance she can't pass up to show off to her employees how good she was at what they do. So she goes over to Bob and says that she's the best in the house and she is available. She sits and talks with him. They frolic a bit, giggle a bit, and drink a little, and she sits in his lap.

And Bob leans forward and whispers in her ear, 'Can I pay in Canadian dollars?'

Bumper Stickers for Seniors:

- Ashmore & Dolittle: Retirement planning and consultants
- Young at heart – slightly older in other places
- Don't worry about your health – it will go away.
- I'm retired. I was tired yesterday. I'm tired again today.
- Goodbye tensions – Hello pension!
- Live each day as if it's your last – One day you'll get it right!
- Life is easy – it's freaking people that make it difficult.
- In dog years – I'm dead.
- I always cook with wine – and sometimes add it to the food.
- Geezer – (gee-zer – noun) slang. Not young. Not dead. Somewhere in between.
- I don't think about dying – that's the last thing I want to do.

- I'm speeding because I have to get there before I forget where I'm going.
- I don't exercise – it makes my coffee spill.
- I just can't get started in the morning until I've had a piping-hot pot of coffee in the morning. Oh, I've tried other enemas.
- At my age – 'getting any' means sleep.
- Eat right and exercise – die anyway.
- Be nice to your kids – they will pick your nursing home.
- I believe in having sex on the first date – At my age – there might not be a second.
- The only trouble with retirement is that you never get a day off.

True or False?

1. Apples, not caffeine, are more efficient at waking you up in the morning.
2. Alfred Hitchcock didn't have a belly button.
3. People do not get sick from cold weather; it's from being indoors a lot more.
4. The toothbrush was invented in 1498.
5. The average housefly lives for one month.
6. The average computer user blinks seven times a minute.
7. Most of us have eaten a spider in our sleep.
8. Michael Jackson owned the rights to the South Carolina State Anthem.
9. The first Harley Davidson motorcycle built in 1903 used a tomato can for a carburettor.
10. Humphrey Bogart was related to Princess Diana.
11. The average person over fifty will have spent five years waiting in lines.
12. Your feet are bigger in the afternoon than any other time of the day.
13. The only two animals that can see behind themselves without turning their heads are the rabbit and the parrot.
14. John Travolta turned down the starring roles in 'An Officer and a Gentleman' and 'Tootsie.'

15. In most television commercials advertising milk, a mixture of white paint and a little thinner is used in place of the milk.
16. Only seven percent of the population are lefties.
17. When you sneeze, all bodily functions stop – even your heart.
18. 40,000 Americans are injured by toilets each year.
19. The coat hanger is 1.73 metres long when straightened.

They are all true. Now go back and think about #7.

CHAPTER 14

MISCELLANEOUS

What a coincidence:

A farmer went to a local bar and ordered a glass of champagne. The woman sitting next to him said, 'How about that? I just ordered champagne too!'

'What a coincidence, the farmer said. 'This is a special day for me so I'm celebrating.'

'So am I,' she replied.

As they clinked glasses he added, 'What are you celebrating?'

'My husband and I have been trying to have a child and today my gynaecologist told me that I'm pregnant!'

'What a coincidence,' said the farmer, 'I'm a chicken farmer and all the past year my hens were infertile, but today they started laying eggs again.'

'That's great,' said the woman, 'How did the hens become fertile?'

'I used a different cock,' he replied.

'What a coincidence,' the woman replied as they again clinked glasses.

Natural born citizens:

I don't know whether to laugh or cry. Here is the real problem:

In a Canadian university classroom, they were discussing the qualifications to be Prime Minister of Canada. It was pretty simple. The candidate must be a natural born citizen of at least thirty-five years of age.

However, one girl in the class immediately started in on how unfair was the requirement to be a natural born citizen.

In short, her opinion was that this requirement prevented many capable individuals from becoming Prime Minister. The class was taking it in and letting her rant, and not many jaws hit the floor when she wrapped up her argument by stating, 'What makes a natural born citizen any more qualified to lead this country than one born by C-section?'

Yep, these are the same kinds of kids that are now voting in our elections! They breed and they walk amongst us.

Business Names:

The owners of these businesses deserve a standing ovation for these names:

- Taquila Mockingbird (bar)
- Papa Razzi (restaurant)
- Florist Gump (florist)
- Luna Sea Motel
- Curl up and Dye
- Nin Com Soup (restaurant)
- Shear Lock Combs
- Cycloanalysts (bicycle shop)
- I'll cut you (hairdresser)
- Deja Brew (pub)
- YahPoo Plumbing
- Thistle do Nicely (room rentals)
- Lawn & Order (property maintenance)
- Indiana Bones Temple of Groom (Doggy day care & Boutique)
- Jerassic Pork (mobile canteen)
- Sherlock Homes (locksmith)
- Carl's Pane in the Glass (window repair)
- Attitude Adjustment Shoppe (wine & liquor shop)

Urine or you're out!

I have a job. I work, they pay me. I pay my taxes and the government distributes my taxes as it sees fit. In order to get that pay cheque, in my case, I am required to pass a random urine test (with which I have no problem). What I do have a problem with is the distribution of my taxes to people who don't have to pass a urine test.

So, here is my question: Shouldn't one have to pass a urine test to get a dole payment, because I have to pass one to earn it for them? Please understand, I have no problem with helping people get back on their feet. I do, on the other hand, have a problem with helping someone sitting on their backside doing drugs while I work.

Can you imagine how much money we would save if people had to pass a urine test to get a dole payment? I guess we could call the program 'Urine or you're out!'

Chinese Torture

A young man was wandering, lost in a forest, when he came upon a small house. Knocking on the door, he was greeted by an ancient Chinese man with a long, grey beard.

'I'm lost,' said the man. 'Can you put me up for the night?'

'Certainly,' the Chinese man said, 'but on one condition. If you so much as lay a finger on my daughter I will inflict upon you the three worst Chinese tortures known to man.'

'Okay,' said the man, thinking that the daughter must be pretty old as well, and entered the house.

Before dinner, the daughter came down the stairs. She was young, beautiful and had a fantastic figure. She was obviously attracted to the young man as she couldn't keep her eyes off him during the meal.

Remembering the old man's warning, he ignored her and went up to bed alone. But during the night he could bear it no longer and snuck into her room for a night of passion. He was careful to keep everything quiet so the old man wouldn't hear and, near dawn, he crept back to his room, exhausted but happy.

He woke to feel a pressure on his chest. Opening his eyes, he saw a large rock on his chest with a note on it that read, 'Chinese Torture 1: Large rock on chest.'

'Well, that's pretty crappy,' he thought. 'If that's the best the old man can do then I don't have much to worry about.'

He picked the boulder up, walked over to the window and threw the boulder out. As he did so he noticed another note on it that read, 'Chinese Torture 2: Rock tied to left testicle.'

In a panic he glanced down and saw the line that was already getting close to taut. Figuring that a few broken bones was better than castration, he jumped out of the window after the boulder. As he plummeted downward he saw a large sign on the ground that read, 'Chinese Torture 3: Right testicle tied to bedpost.'

Irish jokes:

- Bloke at a horse race whispers to Paddy next to him, 'Do you want the winner of the next race?'

    Paddy replies 'No tanks, Oi've only got a small yard.'

- Paddy and Mick found three hand grenades and decided to take them to the police station.

    Mick 'What if one explodes before we get there?

    Paddy: 'We'll lie and say we only found two!'

- A coach load of paddies on a mystery tour decided to run a sweepstake to guess where they were going. The driver won £52!

- Paddy finds a sandwich with two wires stickin out of it. He phones the police and says 'Bejasus I've just found a sandwich dat looks like a bomb.'

    The operator asks, 'Is it tickin?'

    Paddy says 'No, Oi tink it's beef.'

- Mick walks into Paddy's barn and catches him dancing naked in front of a tractor.

    Mick says, 'Oi Paddy, what ya doing?'

    Paddy says, 'Well me and Mary haven't been getting on in the bedroom lately and the therapist recommended I do something sexy to a tractor.'

- The Irish have solved their own fuel problems. They imported 50 million tonnes of sand from the Arabs and they're going to drill for their own oil.

- Paddy says to Mick, 'Christmas is on a Friday this year.'

    Mick says 'Let's hope it's not the 13th.'

- Paddy's in the bathroom and Murphy shouts to him. 'Did you find the shampoo?'

    Paddy says, 'Oi did, but it's for dry hair and I've just wet mine.'

Stormy Night:

John Bradford, a Dublin University student, was on the side of the road hitchhiking on a very dark night and in the midst of a big storm. The night was rolling on and no car went by. The storm was so strong, he could hardly see a few feet ahead of him.

Suddenly, he saw a car slowly coming towards him and stopped. John, desperate for shelter and without thinking about it, got into the car and closed the door, only to realize there was nobody behind the wheel and the engine wasn't on.

The car started moving slowly. John looked at the road ahead and saw a curve approaching. Scared, he started to pray, begging for his life. Then just before the car hit the curve, a hand appeared out of nowhere through the window, and turned the wheel.

John, paralyzed with terror, watched as the hand came through the window, but never touched or harmed him.

Shortly thereafter, John saw the lights of a pub appear down the road, so gathering strength, he jumped out of the car and ran to it. Wet and out of breath, he rushed inside and started telling everybody about the horrible experience he'd just had.

A silence enveloped the pub when everybody realized he was crying – and he wasn't drunk.

Suddenly, the door opened, and two other people walked in from the dark and stormy night. They like John, were soaked and out of breath. Looking around and seeing John sobbing at the bar, one said to the other, 'Look Paddy – there's the idiot that got in the car while we were pushing it!'

To an intelligent friend:

Question: Keep that brain working; see if you can figure out what these seven words all have in common?

1. Banana
2. Dresser
3. Grammar
4. Potato
5. Revive
6. Uneven
7. Assess

Look at each word carefully. You'll kick yourself when you discover the answer.

No, it is not that they all have at least two double letters...

Answer: In all of the words listed, if you take the first letter, place it at the end of the word, and then spell the word backwards, it will be the same word.

Q: Where do you find giant snails?
A: On the ends of giant's fingers.

Q: What did the cannibal get when he was late for dinner?
A: The cold shoulder.

Q: Did you hear about the shoe factory that burnt down?
A: Two hundred soles were lost.

This 'N That:

- If you don't swear while driving, then you're not paying attention to the road at all!
- I heard a rumour that since water was found on the Red Planet, Bundaberg Distillery has sent sugar cane to be planted on a 50 hectare site. Won't be long before rum will be available in a Mars Bar. (D.C. Bond).
- Life is better when you're happy, but life is best when other people are happy because of you.
- What do Alexander the Great and Kermit the Frog have In common? Their middle names.
- Those who live by the sword get shot by those that don't.
- What are the two things you can't have for dinner? Lunch and breakfast.
- What stays hot in the fridge? Mustard.
- What has bread on both sides and is afraid of everything? A chicken sandwich.
- The more you weigh – the harder you are to kidnap – so stay safe and eat cake.
- There are three kinds of people in the world. Those who can count and those that can't.
- Sometimes, when you cry – no one sees your tears. Sometimes, when you're in pain – no one sees your hurt. Sometimes, when you're worried – no one sees your stress. Sometimes, when you're happy – no one sees your smile. But fart just one time – and everybody knows!
- A qualified meteorologist was having a terrible run forecasting the weather for the nightly TV news bulletin. Night after night his predictions for the weather

the following day turned out to be wrong. Eventually he was fired and he moved to a different city where he applied for another job as a TV weather presenter.

At the interview, he was asked why he left his previous job and he replied, 'Because the climate didn't agree with me.'

- When my husband and I arrived at an automobile dealership to pick up our car, we were told the keys had been locked in it. We went to the service department and found a mechanic working feverishly to unlock the driver's side door. As I watched from the passenger side, I instinctively tried the door handle and discovered that it was unlocked.

'Hey,' I announced to the technician, 'It's open!'

To which he replied, 'I know – I already got that side.

(Must have been a male blonde!)

- A man's car stalls on a country road. When he gets out to fix it, a horse in the nearby field comes up along the fence and leans over him.

'Your trouble is probably in the carburettor,' says the horse.

Startled, the man jumps back and runs down the road until he meets a farmer. He tells him his story.

'Was it a large white horse with a black mark over the right eye?' asks the farmer.

'Yes, yes,' the man replies.

'Oh, I wouldn't listen to her,' says the farmer, 'she doesn't know anything about cars.'

- A man was walking down the road leading a horse and saw his mate. His mate said to him, 'What are you going to do with that horse?'

The first man replied, 'Race it.'

The second man then said, 'Well, by the looks of it, you will win!'
- How do astronomers organize a party? They planet.
- A small frog goes to a fortune teller and asks if he is going to meet a young girl.

The fortune teller says, 'Yes, you are.'

The frog replies, 'Where? In a pub or at a party?'

The fortune teller replies, 'In biology class.'

Lesson of Time:

When a bird is alive, it eats ants. When the bird is dead, ants eat the bird.

Time and circumstances can change at any time. Don't devalue or hurt anyone in life. You may be more powerful today, but remember – time is more powerful than you.

One tree makes a million match sticks, but only one match stick is needed to burn millions of trees. So be good and do good.

Po Taters

- Some people never seem motivated to participate, but are just content to watch while others do the work. They are called 'Spec Taters.'
- Some people never do anything to help, but are gifted at finding fault with the way others do the work. They are called 'Comment Taters.'
- Some people are very bossy and like to tell others what to do, but don't want to soil their own hands. They are called 'Dick Taters.'
- Some people are always looking to cause problems by asking others to agree with them. It is too hot or too cold, too sour or to sweet. They're called 'Agie Taters.'
- There are those who say they will help, but somehow just never get around to actually doing the promised help. They are called 'Hezzie Taters.'

- Some people can put up a front and pretend to be someone they are not. They are called 'Immy Taters.'
- Then there are those who love others and do what they say they will. They are always prepared to stop whatever they're doing and lend a helping hand. They bring real sunshine into the lives of others. They are called 'Sweet Po Taters.'

The Golfer:

A circus owner runs an ad for a lion tamer and two people show up. One is a golfer in his seventies, the other a drop-dead gorgeous brunette with a great body in her twenties.

The circus owner tells them 'I'm not going to sugar coat it. This is one ferocious lion. He ate my last tamer so you two had better be good or you're history. Here's your equipment – a chair, a whip and a gun. Who wants to try out first?'

The gorgeous brunette says, 'I'll go first.'

She walks past the chair, the whip and the gun and steps right into the lion's cage. The lion gets all heated up, starts to snarl and pant and begins to charge her. As he gets close, the gorgeous brunette throws open her coat, revealing her beautiful, perfect, naked body. The lion stops dead in his tracks, sheepishly crawls up to her and starts licking her feet and ankles. He continues to lick and kiss every inch of her body for several minutes, then lays down and rests his head at her feet.'

The circus owner's jaw is on the floor. He says, 'That's amazing! I've never seen anything like that in my life!'

Then he turns to the golfer and asks, 'Can you top that?'

The tough old golfer replies 'Possibly... but you've got to get that lion out of there first.'

Vagabond:

An eighteenth-century vagabond in England, exhausted and famished, came to a roadside Inn with a sign reading:

'George and the Dragon.' He knocked. The innkeeper's wife stuck her head out a window.

'Could ye spare some victuals?' he asked.

The woman glanced at his shabby, dirty clothes. 'No!' she shouted.

'Could I have a pint of ale?'

'No!' she shouted.

'Could I at least sleep in your stable?'

'No!' she shouted again.

The vagabond said, 'Might I please…?'

'What now?' the woman screeched, not allowing him to finish.

'D'ye suppose,' he asked, 'that I might have a word with George?'

The opportunist:

Dear Optimist, Pessimist and Realist,

While you guys were busy arguing about the glass of water, I drank it.

Sincerely, the Opportunist.

Golden Syrup

A man with a bald head and a wooden leg is invited to a Christmas fancy dress party. He doesn't know what to wear to hide his head and his wooden leg, so he writes to a fancy dress company to explain his problem. A few days later he receives a parcel with a note:

Dear Sir,

Please find enclosed a Pirate's outfit. The spotted handkerchief will cover your bald head and with your wooden leg you will be just right as a Pirate.

The man is offended that the outfit emphasizes his disability, so he writes a letter of complaint. A week passes and he receives another parcel and note:

Dear Sir,

Sorry about the previous parcel. Please find enclosed a monk's habit. The long robe will cover your wooden leg and with your bald head you will really look the part.

The man is really incandescent with rage now, because the company has gone from emphasizing his wooden leg to drawing attention to his bald head. So he writes a really strong letter of complaint.

A few days later he gets a very small parcel from the company with the accompanying letter:

Dear Sir,

Please find enclosed a tin of Golden Syrup. We suggest you pour the tin of Golden Syrup over your bald head, let it harden, then stick your wooden leg up your arse and go as a toffee apple.

Unfortunate headlines from around the world:

- Stolen painting found by a tree.
- Lung cancer in women mushrooms.
- Dealers will hear car talk at noon.
- Miners refuse to work after death.
- Milk drinkers are turning to powder.
- Safety experts say school bus passengers should be belted.
- Two sisters reunited after 18 years at checkout counter.
- Grandmother of eight makes hole in one.
- Red tape holds up new bridge.
- Squad helps dog bite victim.

Turkey jokes:

- Q: Why can't you take a turkey to church?

- A: They use fowl language.
- Q: What do you get when you cross a turkey with a banjo?
- A: A turkey that can pluck itself!
- Q: What key has legs and can't open doors?
- A: A Turkey.
- Q: What sound does a turkey's phone make?
- A: Wing! Wing!
- Q: Who doesn't eat on Thanksgiving?
- A: A turkey because it is always stuffed.
- Q: If the Pilgrims were alive today, what would they be most famous for?
- A: Their age!
- Q: Why did the cow go in the spaceship?
- A: It wanted to see the mooooooon!
- Q: How do chickens get strong?
- A: Egg-cersize.

The Squirrels:

There were five places of worship in a small Ohio town: a Presbyterian church, a Baptist church, a Methodist church, a Catholic church and a Jewish synagogue. Each church and the synagogue had a problem with squirrels.

The Presbyterian church called a meeting to decide what to do about their squirrels. After much prayer and consideration, they determined the squirrels were predestined to be there and they shouldn't interfere with God's divine will.

At the Baptist church the squirrels had taken an interest in the baptistery. The deacons met and decided to put a water slide on the baptistery and let the squirrels drown themselves. The squirrels liked the slide and, unfortunately, knew instinctively how to swim so twice as many squirrels showed up the following week.

The Methodist church decided that they were not in a position to harm any of God's creatures. So, they humanely trapped their squirrels and set them free near the Baptist Church. Two weeks later the squirrels were back when the Baptists took down the water slide.

But the Catholic Church came up with a very creative strategy. They baptized all the squirrels and consecrated them as members of the church. Now they only see them on Christmas and Easter.

Not much was heard from the Jewish synagogue, but it's rumoured that they took one squirrel and circumcised him and they haven't seen a squirrel on their property since.

CHAPTER 15

HISTORY

Japan - some interesting facts

- In just ten years Hiroshima returned to what it was - economically vibrant before the fall of the atomic bomb.
- Japan prevents the use of mobile phones in trains, restaurants and indoors.
- For first to sixth primary year Japanese students must learn ethics in dealing with people.
- Even though one of the richest people in the world, the Japanese do not have servants. The parents are responsible for the house and children.
- There is no examination from the first to the third primary level because the goal of education is to instill concepts and character building.
- If you go to a buffet restaurant in Japan, you will notice people only eat as much as they need without any waste because food must not be wasted.
- The rate of delayed trains in Japan is about 7 seconds per year! The Japanese appreciate the value of time and are very punctual.

Japan is a country keeping Islam at bay by putting strict restrictions on Islam and all Muslims.

1) Japan is the only nation that does not give citizenship to Muslims.
2) In Japan permanent residency is not given to Muslims.
3) There is a strong ban on the propagation of Islam in Japan.
4) In the University of Japan, Arabic or any Islamic language is not taught.
5) One cannot import a 'Koran' published in the Arabic language.

6) According to data published by the Japanese government, it has given temporary residency to only 2 lakhs, Muslims, who must follow the Japanese Law of the Land. These Muslims should speak Japanese and carry their religious rituals in their homes.
7) Japan is the only country in the world that has a negligible number of embassies in Islamic countries.
8) Muslims residing in Japan are the employees of foreign companies.
9) Even today, visas are not granted to Muslim doctors, engineers or managers sent by foreign companies.
10) In the majority of companies, it is stated in their regulations that no Muslims should apply for a job.
11) The Japanese government is of the opinion that Muslims are fundamentalist, and even in the era of globalization they are not willing to change their Muslim laws.
12) Muslims cannot even rent a house in Japan.
13) If anyone comes to know that his neighbor is a Muslim then the whole neighborhood stays alert.
14) No one can start an Islamic cell or Arabic 'Madrasa' in Japan.
15) There is no Sharia law in Japan.
16) If a Japanese woman marries a Muslim, she is considered an outcast forever.

The Japanese might have lost WWII, but they are in charge of their own country. There are no bombs going off in crowded business centers, 'Honor Killings' nor killing of innocent children or anyone else.

Something to think about.

1915:

What a difference a century makes!

Here are some statistics for the Year 1915:

- The average life expectancy for men was 47 years.
- Fuel for cars was sold in drug stores only.

- Only 14 percent of the homes had a bathtub.
- Only 8 percent of the homes had a telephone.
- The maximum speed limit in most cities was 10 mph.
- The tallest structure in the world was the Eiffel Tower.
- The average US wage in 1910 was 22 cents per hour.
- The average US worker made between $200 and $400 per year...
- A competent accountant could expect to earn $2,000 per year.
- A dentist $2,500 per year.
- A veterinarian between $1,500 and $4,000 per year.
- And, a mechanical engineer about $5,000 per year.
- More than 95 percent of all births took place at home.
- Ninety percent of all Doctors had no college education! Instead, they attended so-called medical schools, many of which were condemned in the press and the government as "substandard.'
- Sugar cost four cents a pound. Eggs were fourteen cents a dozen.
- Coffee was fifteen cents a pound.
- Most women only washed their hair once a month and, used Borax or egg yolks for shampoo.
- Canada passed a law that prohibited poor people from entering into their country for any reason.

The Five leading causes of death were:

1. Pneumonia and influenza
2. Tuberculosis
3. Diarrhea
4. Heart disease
5. Stroke

The American flag had 45 stars...

The population of Las Vegas, Nevada was only 30.

Crossword puzzles, canned beer and iced tea hadn't been invented yet.

There was neither a Mother's Day nor a Father's Day.

Two out of every 10 adults couldn't read or write and only 6 percent of all Americans had graduated from high school.

Marijuana, heroin, and morphine were all available over the counter at corner drugstores.

Back then pharmacists said, 'Heroin clears the complexion, gives buoyancy to the mind, regulates the stomach, bowels, and is, in fact, a perfect guardian of health!' (Shocking?)

Eighteen percent of households had at least one full-time servant or domestic help...

There were about 230 reported murders in the entire U.S.A.!

It is impossible to imagine what it may be like in another 100 years. The way the world is going I wonder if we will make it another 100 years.

Things to know:

- Many years ago in Scotland, a new game was invented. It was ruled 'Gentlemen Only - Ladies Forbidden' and thus, the word GOLF entered into the English language.
- Golf is a game invented by the same people who think music comes out of a bagpipe.
- The first couple to be shown in bed together on prime time TV was Fred and Wilma Flintstone.
- Coca-Cola was originally green.
- The cost of raising a medium-size dog to the age of eleven: £ 10,120.00
- 111,111,111 X 111,111,111 = 12,345,678,987,654,321.
- Mead is a honey beer and because their calendar was lunar based, this period was called the honey month, which we know today as the honeymoon.
- Never be afraid to try something new. Remember that a lone amateur built the Ark. A large group of professionals built the Titanic.

- Gone are the days when girls used to cook like their mothers. Now they drink like their fathers.
- You cannot hang out with negative people and expect to live a positive life.
- I don't believe it's age that makes us forgetful, it's having way too many stupid things to remember!

You know you are living in 2016 when...

1. Your reason for not staying in touch with friends and family is that they don't have e-mail addresses.
2. Every commercial on television has a web site at the bottom of the screen
3. Leaving the house without your mobile phone, which you didn't even have the first 20 or 30 (or 60) years of your life, is now a cause for panic and you turn around to go and get it
4. You get up in the morning and go on line, before getting your coffee
5. You start tilting your head sideways to smile. :)

Famous words:

- 'It's not the strongest of the species that survive, nor the most intelligent that survives. It's the one that is most adaptable to change' Charles Darwin.
- 'Big news from the Oxford English Dictionary. For all of you kids who don't know what a dictionary is, it's a small portion of the Internet, printed out, kept on a shelf and opened once every three years during a Scrabble game.' - Jimmy Kimmel.
- 'As I hurtled through space, one thought kept crossing my mind - every part of this rocket was supplied by the lowest bidder' - John Glenn.
- 'When the white missionaries came to Africa they had the Bible and we had the land. They said 'Let us pray.' We closed our eyes. When we opened them we had the Bible and they had the land.' - Desmond Tutu.

- 'America is the only country where a significant proportion of the population believes that professional wrestling is real but the moon landing was faked.' – David Letterman.
- 'After the game, the King and the pawn go into the same box.' – Old Italian proverb.
- 'When a man opens a car door for his wife, it's either a new car or a new wife.' – Prince Philip.
- 'Wood burns faster when you have to cut and chop it yourself.' – Harrison Ford.
- 'The best cure for sea sickness, is to sit under a tree.' – Spike Milligan.
- 'Lawyers believe a person is innocent until proven broke.' – Robin Hall.
- 'A pessimist sees the difficulty in every opportunity; an optimist sees the opportunity in every difficulty.' – Winston S. Churchill.
- 'We sleep safely at night because rough men stand ready to visit violence on those who would harm us.' – Winston S. Churchill.
- 'I contend that for a nation to try to tax itself into prosperity is like a man standing in a bucket and trying to lift himself up by the handle.' – Winston S. Churchill.
- 'The military don't start wars. Politicians start wars.' – William C. Westmoreland.
- 'For those who have fought for it, freedom has a flavour the protected will never know. – A soldier.
- 'You will never find a rainbow if you're looking down.' – Charles Chaplin.
- 'Kill one man and you're a murderer, kill a million and you're a conqueror.' – Jean Rostand.
- 'Having more money doesn't make you happier. I have 50 million dollars but I'm just as happy as when I had 48 million.' – Arnold Schwarzenegger.
- 'We are here on earth to do good unto others. What the others are here for, I have no idea.' – W.H. Auden.

- 'If life were fair, Elvis would still be alive today and all the impersonators would be dead.' – Jonny Carson.
- 'Hollywood must be the only place on earth where you can be fired by a man wearing a Hawaiian shirt and a baseball cap.' Steve Martin.
- 'Home cooking. Where many a man thinks his wife is.' – Jimmy Durante.
- 'A government is like a baby's alimentary canal, with a happy appetite at one end and no responsibility at the other.' – Ronald Reagan.
- 'In general, the art of government consists of taking as much money as possible from one party of the citizens to give to the other.' – Voltaire (1764)
- 'What this country needs are more unemployed politicians.' – Edward Langley, Artist (1928-1995)
- 'A government big enough to give you everything you want, is strong enough to take everything you have.' – Thomas Jefferson.
- 'The first piece of luggage on the carousel never belongs to anyone.' – George Roberts.
- 'If God had intended us to fly he would have made it easier to get to the airport.' – Jonathan Winters.
- 'I have kleptomania, but when it gets bad, I take something for it.' – Robert Benchley.
- 'Sometimes you need to keep your feelings to yourself because you can find no language to describe them.' - Jane Austin.
- 'When the power of love overcomes the love of power, the world will know peace.' - Jimi Hendrix.
- 'Some people think football is a matter of life and death… I can assure them it is much more serious than that.' – Bill Shankly.
- 'In my many years I have come to a conclusion that one useless man is a shame, two is a law firm and three or more is a government.' – John Adams.

- 'Paradise would be a place where everybody has guaranteed employment, free comprehensive healthcare, free education, free food, free housing, free clothing, free utilities and only law enforcement has guns. And believe it or not – such a place does indeed already exist: It's called Prison.' – Sheriff Joe Arpaio, Marcopa County, Arizona.
- 'It's only when you see a mosquito landing on your testicles that you realize there is always a way to solve problems without using violence.' – Leo Tzu.
- 'Whenever you see a successful person, you only see the public glories, never the private sacrifices to reach them.' - Vaibhau Shah
- 'Those who think they know it all, have no way of finding out they don't.' – Leo Buscaglia.
- 'Football is not a contact sport; it's a collision sport – dancing is a contact sport.' – Vince Lombasrdi.

Unknown Quotes:

- 'If you can read this, thank a teacher. Since you are reading it in English, thank a veteran'
- 'There can be no courage unless you're scared.'
- 'The only thing necessary for triumph of evil is for good men to do nothing.'
- 'It's better to walk alone, than with a crowd going in the wrong direction.'
- 'If a cluttered desk is a sign of a cluttered mind, of what, then, is an empty desk a sign?'
- 'Some people are old at 18 and some are young at 90. Time is a concept that humans created.'
- 'The most destructive force in the universe is gossip.'
- 'Some people change your life by coming into it, others change it by going out!'
- 'A society grows great when old men plant trees whose shade they know they'll never sit it.'

The pawnbroker:

King Ozymandias of Assyria was running low on cash after years of war with the Hittites. His last great possession was the Star of the Euphhrates, the most valuable diamond in the ancient world. Desperate, he went to Croesus, the pawnbroker to ask for a loan.

Croesus said, 'I'll give you 100,000 dinars for it.'

'But I paid a million dinars for it,' the King protested. 'Don't you know who I am? I am the king!'

Croesus replied, 'When you wish to pawn a Star, it makes no difference who you are.'

(I heard you groan...)

Armed Service Jokes:

At a regimental dinner, 'Tonight we honour a man who doesn't know the meaning of fear; a man who doesn't know the meaning of defeat, quit or surrender. So we have all chipped in and bought him a dictionary.'

'Sorry for not calling you last New Year's Eve, but I've just got out of jail. I was locked up for punching out this idiot at a party. In my defense, when you hear an Arab counting down from ten, your instincts kick in.'

When Fred joined the Return Servicemen's Club, they asked him if he had a war record. He replied, 'Bloody oath I have. I've got Vera Lynn singing the White Cliffs of Dover.'

There are three types of intelligence: the intelligence of man, the intelligence of animals and the intelligence of the military... in that order.

At a camp, the Colonel calls the Captain: 'take as many soldiers as you need and start building additional latrines. The number of troops in need has increased!'

The Captain replies, 'I would suggest sir, instead of building more latrines, maybe you should just get a new cook!'

At Ranwick Army camp, the trip to the rifle range had been cancelled, but the physical fitness test was still on as planned. One recruit mused, 'Does it bother anyone else that the Army doesn't seem to care how well we can shoot, but they're extremely interested in how fast we can run?'

While landing at night in Vietnam, a helicopter pilot messes up and lands on its tail rotor. The landing is so hard it breaks off the tail boom. However, the chopper fortunately remains upright on its skids, sliding down the runway, doing 360s. As the Huey slides past the tower, training a brilliant shower of sparks, this radio exchange takes place:

Tower: 'Sir do you need any assistance?'

Pilot: 'I don't know mate, I ain't done crashin' yet.'

The reunions:

A group of veterans, all aged 40, discussed where they should meet for their ten-year Army Reunion luncheon. Finally, it was agreed that they would meet at the Highway Pub because the waitresses had big breasts and wore mini-skirts.

Ten years later, at age 50, the friends again discussed where they would meet for the next tenth-year celebration. They agreed they would meet at the same pub because the food and service was good and the beer selection was excellent.

Ten years later, at age 60, the friends again discussed where they would meet for the next tenth-year celebration. They agreed they would meet at the same pub because there was plenty of parking, they could dine in peace and quiet, and it was good value for money.

Ten years later, at age 70, the friends again discussed where they would meet for the next tenth-year celebration. They agreed they would meet at the same pub because the restaurant was wheelchair accessible and had a toilet for the disabled.

Ten years later, at age 80, the friends again discussed where they would meet for the next tenth-year celebration. They agreed they would meet at the same pub because they had never been there before.

Mae West:

She was quite a gal! Here are some of her beliefs:

- Good sex is like playing a good game of bridge. If you don't have a good partner you had better have a good hand.'
- 'Give a man a free hand and he will run it all over you.'
- 'I used to be Snow White, but I drifted.'
- 'I feel like a million tonight - but one at a time please.'
- 'It's better to be looked over than overlooked.'
- 'When a girl goes wrong, men go right after her.'
- 'Is that a gun in your pocket or are you just glad to see me?'
- 'Between two evils, I always pick the one I haven't tried before.'
- 'It's not the men in my life that counts; it's the life in my men.'
- 'I always say, keep a diary and one day it will keep you.'
- 'When I'm good I'm very very good, and when I'm bad I'm never better.'
- 'A little hush money can do a lot of talking.'
- 'I've been on more laps than a table napkin.'
- 'I don't know a lot about politics but I'd recognize a good party man when I see one.'
- 'A curve is the loveliest distance between two points.'
- 'You must get out of those wet clothes and into a dry martini.'

- 'Too much of a good thing can be wonderful.'

More Interesting Facts:

A shot of whisky: In the old west a .45 cartridge for a six-gun cost 12 cents, so did a shot glass of whisky. If a cowhand was low on cash, he would often give the bartender a cartridge in exchange for a drink. This became known as a 'shot' of whisky.

The whole nine yards: American fighter planes in WWII had machine guns that were fed by a belt of cartridges. The average plane held belts that were 27 feet (that is 9 yards) long. If the pilot used up all his ammo, he was said to have given it the whole nine yards.

Buying the farm: This is synonymous with dying. During WWI, soldiers were given life insurance policies worth $5,000. This was about the price of an average farm, so if a soldier died, he 'bought the farm' for his survivors.

Iron-clad contract: This term came about from the ironclad ships of the Civil War. It meant something so strong that it could not be broken.

Passing the buck/The buck stops here: Most men in the early west carried a jack knife made by the Buck Knife Company. When playing poker, it was common to place one of these Buck Knives in front of the dealer so that everyone knew who he was. When it was time for a new dealer, the deck of cards and the knife were given to the new dealer. If this person didn't want to deal, he would 'pass the buck' to the next player. If that player accepted, then 'the buck stopped here.'

Riff raff: The Mississippi River was the main way of traveling from north to south. Riverboats carried passengers and freight, but the cost was expensive, so most people used rafts. All other boats had the right of way over rafts, which were considered cheap. The steering oar on the rafts was called a 'riff,' and this transposed into riff-raff, meaning low class.

Cobweb: The Old English word for 'spider' was 'cob.'

Ship staterooms: Travelling by steamboat was considered the height of comfort. Passenger cabins on the boats were not numbered. Instead, they were named after states. To this day, cabins on ships are called staterooms.

Sleep tight: Early beds were made with a wooden frame. Ropes were tied across the frame in a criss-cross pattern. A straw mattress was then put on top of the ropes. Over time, the ropes stretched, causing the bed to sag. The owner would then have to tighten the ropes to get a better night's sleep.

Showboat: These were floating theatres built on a barge that was pushed by a steamboat. The showboats played small towns along the Mississippi River. Unlike the boat shown in the movie 'Showboat,' these showboats did not have an engine. They were gaudy and attention-grabbing, which is why we say that someone who is being the life of the party is 'showboating.'

Over a barrel: In the days before CPR, a drowning victim would be placed face down over a barrel, which would be rolled back and forth in an effort to empty the lungs of water. It was rarely effective. If you are over a barrel, you are in deep trouble.

Barge in: Heavy freight was moved along the Mississippi in large barges pushed by steamboats. These were hard to control and would sometimes swing into piers or other boats, so people would say that they 'barged in.'

Hogwash: Steamboats carried both people and animals. Since pigs smelled so badly, they would be washed before being put on board. The mud and other filth that was washed off was considered useless 'hog wash.'

Curfew: The word 'curfew' comes from the French phrase 'couvre-feu,' which means 'cover the fire.' It was used to describe the time of blowing out all lamps and candles. The term was later adopted into Middle English as 'curfeu,' which later became the modern word 'curfew.' In the early American colonies, homes had no real fireplaces, so a fire was built in the centre of the room. To ensure that a fire did not get out of control during the night, it was required that, by an agreed upon time, all fires would be covered with a clay pot called a 'curfew.'

Barrels of oil: When the first oil wells were drilled, oil drillers had made no provision for storing the liquid, so they used water barrels. That is why, to this day, we speak of barrels of oil rather than gallons.

Hot off the press: As the newspaper goes through the rotary printing press, friction causes it to heat up. Therefore, if you grabbed the paper right off the press, it was hot. The expression means to get immediate information.

General Trivia

- A giraffe can clean its ears with its 21-inch tongue. It can go without water longer than a camel can.
- A hedgehog's heart beats 300 times a minute on average.
- A jellyfish is 95 percent water.
- 'Dreamt' is the only English word that ends in the letters 'mt.'
- David Prowse was the guy in the Darth Vader suit in Star Wars. He spoke all of Vader's lines, and didn't know that he was going to be dubbed over by James Earl Jones until he saw the screening of the movie.'
- Until 1965, driving was done on the left-hand side on roads in Sweden. The conversion to right-hand was done on a weekday at 5:00 pm. All traffic stopped as people switched sides. This time and day were chosen to prevent accidents where drivers would have gotten up in the morning and been too sleepy to realize that this was the day of the changeover.

- Niagara Falls actually stopped flowing back in 1848 for about 20 hours because there was ice blocking the Niagara River.
- The flatulation from domestic cows produce about 30% of the methane on this planet.
- The Angels Falls in Venezuela were named after an American pilot, Jimmy Angel, whose plane got stuck on top of the mountain while searching for gold.
- Every second there are 418 Kit Kat fingers eaten in the world.
- Chewing gum has rubber as an ingredient.
- An orca whale can hold its breath for up to 15 minutes.
- In ancient Rome, when a man testified in court he would swear on his privates.
- You can only smell 1/20th as well as a dog.
- You'll eat about 35,000 biscuits in a lifetime.
- You're more likely to get stung by a bee on a windy day than in any other weather.
- There are 318,979,564,000 possible combinations of the first four moves in Chess.
- 'Jedi' is an official religion in Australia with over 70,000 followers.
- The blue whale can produce the loudest sound of any animal. At 188 decibels, the noise can be detected over 800 kilometres away.
- Registered in 1985, symbolics.com is the first ever internet domain registered.
- Coffee beans aren't beans; they are fruit pits.
- The chemical name for caffeine is 1,3,7-trimethyl-zantihine.
- Tomato sauce is a good conditioner for the hair. It also helps get the greenish tinge that some blonde-haired people get after swimming in water with chlorine in it.
- The longest recorded flight of a chicken is thirteen seconds.
- A crocodile cannot stick its tongue out.

- Hershey's Kisses are called that because the machine that makes them looks as if it's kissing the conveyor belt.
- The ant can lift 50 times its own weight; can pull 30 times its own weight and always falls over on its right side when intoxicated.
- The cigarette lighter was invented before the match.
- Dalmatians and Peter Pan (Wendy) are the only two Disney cartoon features with both parents that are present and don't die throughout the movie.
- A dragonfly has a lifespan of 24 hours.
- A hippo can open its mouth wide enough to fit a four-foot tall child inside.
- Al Capone's business card said he was a used furniture dealer.
- Snails can sleep for three years.
- USA bought Alaska from Russia for 2 cents an acre.
- Ramses II, a pharaoh of Egypt died in 1225 B.C. At the time of his death, he had fathered 96 sons and 60 daughters. (Wow – how many wives did he have to do this?)
- The Simpsons is the longest-running prime-time animated series in television history.
- The Olympic was the sister ship of the Titanic, and she provided twenty-five years of service.
- The average city dog lives approximately three years longer than the average country dog.
- Atari had to bury millions of unsold 'E.T.' game cartridges in a New Mexico desert landfill in 1982.
- The tip of a bullwhip moves so fast that it breaks the sound barrier. The crack of the whip is actually a tiny sonic boom.
- The purpose of tonsils is to destroy foreign substances that are swallowed or breathed in.'
- A rabbit is not able to vomit.
- In a lifetime, the average driver will honk 15,250 times.

- An oyster can change its gender.
- The smallest sovereign entity in the world is the Sovereign Military Order of Malta (S.M.O.M.) It's located in the city of Rome, Italy, has an area of two tennis courts and as of 2001 had a population of 80, 20 less people than the Vatican. It's a sovereign entity under international law, just as the Vatican is.
- Japan has approximately 200 volcanoes and is home to 10% of the active volcanoes in the world.
- Queen Elizabeth always wore a necklace with a little perfume bottle attached everywhere she went.
- A group of people that are hired to clap at a performance are called a claque.
- Polar bear livers contain so much Vitamin A that it can be fatal if eaten by a human.
- Finland is also known as 'the land of the thousand lakes,' because of the over 188,000 lakes found in that country.'
- Canada has more inland waters and lakes than any other country in the world.
- When Kleenex was first introduced to the market in 1924, it was marketed as a make-up or cold cream remover.
- In the year 1900, for women to be a telephone operator she had to be between the ages of 17 and 26 and not be married.
- In 1894, the first big Coke sign was found on the side of a building located in Cartersville, Georgia, and still exists today.
- Colgate faced a big obstacle marketing toothpaste in Spanish-speaking countries. Colgate translates into the command 'go hang yourself.' (Oh dear!)
- Incas used to create pots in the shape of peanuts that were highly prized.
- French soldiers during World War I had the nickname 'poilu' which translates to 'hairy one.'

- The biggest disco ball in the world has a diameter of 2.41 metres and 137.89 kilograms. It also has 6,900 mirror squares on it.
- Nerve impulses for muscle position, travel at a speed of up to 390 feet per second.
- In 1832, in Paisley, Scotland the first municipal water filtration works was opened.
- The average iceberg weighs 20,000,000 tons.
- Irish Wolfhound dogs have a short lifespan of 7-8 years.
- The external tank on space shuttles is not painted. It's the only part of the shuttle that is lost after launch, so it's not necessary to worry about metal corrosion.

Australian Trivia:

- Australia is the largest island and the smallest, flattest continent on earth.
- In land area, Australis is estimated to be 7,692,024 square kilometres and the sixth largest nation after Russia, Canada, China, The United States of America and Brazil.
- Only one in ten Australians uses public transport to get to work and more people walk to work than catch a bus.
- If Australia were a city, at 23.5 million, it would still only be the world's seventh largest city (after Tokyo, Guanzhou, Shanghai, Jakarta, Seoul and Delhi.)
- In 1952, just 40 Australians turned 100. Last year, more than 2600 Australians turned 100.
- Australia is the only continent without an active volcano.
- The average Australian will consume half a tonne of cheese, eight tonnes of fruit and ten tonnes of vegetables.

Australian Pronunciation:

For those born in North America – this might help you understand the Australian language a bit better. They don't pronounce 'r's' at the end of a word:

- better: bettah
- over: ovah
- here: hee-ah
- living room: lounge room
- sofa: lounge
- truck: lorrie or ute
- university: uni
- cookie: bickie
- scone: biscuit
- bathing suit: cozzie
- sunglasses: sunnies
- afternoon: arvo
- trunk; boot
- hood; bonnet
- windshield: windscreen
- tires: tyres
- gas: petrol
- LPG: natural gas
- natural gas: cold stream gas
- asphalt: bitumen
- candy; lollies
- Adidas: ah-deedaz
- controversy: con-traw-va-see
- pregnant: preggy
- baby: bub
- mom: mum
- wallet: purse
- purse: handbag
- hardwood floors: timber floors
- flashlight: torch
- sweater: jumper
- light: globe
- phone (as in phone you): ring
- aluminium: aluminium
- flying foxes - bats

- sales slip: docket
- plastic wrap: cling wrap
- felt pen: biro
- good morning: g'day
- amazed: gobsmacked
- highway: motorway
- papaya: paw paw
- beets: beetroot
- math: maths
- Cairns: Cans

The Last Post:

If any of you have ever been to a military funeral in which 'The Last Post' was played; this brings out a new meaning of it.

We've all heard the haunting song, 'The Last Post.' It's the song that gives us the lump in our throats and usually tears in our eyes. But, do you know the story behind the song? If not, I think you'll be interested to find out about its humble beginnings.

Reportedly, it all began in 1862 during the American Civil War, when Union Army Captain Robert Ellicombe was with his men near Harrison's Landing in Virginia. The Confederate Army was on the other side of the narrow strip of land.

During the night, Captain Ellicombe heard the moans of a soldier who lay severely wounded on the field. Not knowing if it was a Union or Confederate soldier, the Captain decided to risk his life and bring the stricken man back for medical attention. Crawling on his stomach through the gunfire, the Captain reached the stricken soldier and began pulling him toward his encampment.

When the Captain finally reached his own lines, he discovered it was actually a Confederate soldier, but the soldier was dead.

The Captain lit a lantern and suddenly caught his breath and went numb with shock. In the dim light, he saw the face of the soldier. It was his own son. The boy had been studying music in the South when the war broke out. Without telling his father, the boy enlisted in the Confederate Army.

The following morning, heartbroken, the father asked permission of his superiors to give his son a full military burial, despite his enemy status. His request was only partially granted.

The Captain had asked if he could have a group of Army band members play a funeral dirge for his son at the funeral. The request was turned down since the soldier was a Confederate.

But, out of respect for the father, they did say they could give him only one musician.

The Captain chose a bugler. He asked the bugler to play a series of musical notes he'd found on a piece of paper in the pocket of the dead youth's uniform. This wish was granted.

The haunting melody, we now know as 'The Last Post' used at military funerals was born.

I now have an even deeper respect for the song than I did before. Remember those lost and harmed while serving their country.

The Canadian bird feeder:

George bought a bird feeder and hung it on his back porch and lovingly filled it with seeds. Within a week he had hundreds of birds taking advantage of the continuous flow of free and easily accessible food.

However, the birds started building nests in his patio, above the table, under the eaves and next to the barbecue. Then came the shit. It was everywhere: on the patio tile, the chairs, the table, the BBQ... everywhere! Then some of the birds turned mean and some fought each other. They dive-bombed George and tried to peck him even though he had fed them out of his own pocket.

The birds were boisterous and loud. They sat on the feeder and squawked and screamed at all hours of the day and night and demanded that he fill it when the feeder got low on food.

After a while, he couldn't sit on his back porch any more, so he took down the bird feeder and in three days the birds were gone. He cleaned up their mess and took down the many nests they had built all over the patio and the back yard.

Soon, the back yard became quiet, serene and no one demanded their rights to a free meal.

Moral of the story:

Here's a solution for the economic mess that America/Canada/Western Europe in general, but primarily Germany, Holland, Sweden, Austria, the UK and France, to say nothing of Italy and Greece, as well as Australia and New Zealand.

Nowadays our government gives out free food, subsidized housing, free medical care and free education, and allows anyone born here to be an automatic citizen.

Then the illegals came by the tens of thousands. Suddenly taxes went up to pay for free services; small apartments are housing five families; you have to wait six hours to be seen by an emergency room doctor; your child's second grade class is behind other schools because over half the class doesn't speak English and/or French) to point out just a few problems. While I'm venting, not to say anything about our bloated Governments, municipal, provincial and federal and the zillions of unnecessary bureaucrats.

Corn Flakes now come in a bilingual or even trilingual box; I have to 'press one' (or '9' in Quebec) to hear my bank talk to me in English, and people waving flags other than 'ours' are squawking and screaming in the streets, demanding justice and more rights and free liberties, as if liberty ever came free.

Just my opinion, but maybe it's time for the government to take down the bird feeder.

Time Machine:

Barak Obama and David Cameron are shown a time machine which can see one hundred years into the future. They both decide to test it by asking a question each.

Barak goes first. 'What will the USA be like in one hundred years' time?'

The machine whirs and beeps and goes into action and gives him a printout. It reads, 'The country is in the hands of the new president, crime is non-existent, there is no conflict and the economy is healthy. There are no worries.'

David thinks, 'This time machine's not bad, so he asks: 'What will England be like in one hundred years' time?'

The machine whirs and beeps and goes into action and he gets the printout. But he just stares at it.

'Come on David' says Barak, 'What does it say?'

David replies, 'Buggered if I know! It's not in English.'

A message from the Queen:

To the citizens of the United States of America from Her Sovereign Majesty Queen Elizabeth II:

In light of your failure in recent years to nominate competent candidates for President of the USA and thus to govern yourselves, we hereby give notice of the revocation of your independence, effective immediately. (You should look up 'revocation' in the Oxford English Dictionary.)

Her Sovereign Majesty Queen Elizabeth II will resume monarchical duties over all states, commonwealths, and territories (except North Dakota, which she does not fancy).

Your new Prime Minister, David Cameron, will appoint a Governor for America without the need for further elections.

Congress and the Senate will be disbanded. A questionnaire may be circulated next year to determine whether any of you noticed.

To aid in the transition to a British Crown dependency, the following rules are introduced with immediate effect:

1. The letter 'U' will be reinstated in words such as 'colour,' 'favour,' 'labour' and 'neighbour.' Likewise, you will learn to spell 'doughnut' without skipping half the letters, and the suffix '-ize' will be replaced by the suffix '-ise.' Generally, you will be expected to raise your vocabulary to acceptable levels. (Look up 'vocabulary').
2. Using the same twenty-seven words interspersed with filler noises such as "like' and 'you know' is an unacceptable and inefficient form of communication. There is no such thing as U.S. English. We will let Microsoft know on your behalf. The Microsoft spell-checker will be adjusted to take into account the reinstated letter 'u" and the elimination of '-ize.'
3. July 4th will no longer be celebrated as a holiday.
4. You will learn to resolve personal issues without using guns, lawyers, or therapists. The fact that you need so many lawyers and therapists shows that you're not quite ready to be independent. Guns should only be used for shooting grouse. If you can't sort things out without suing someone or speaking to a therapist, then you're not ready to shoot grouse.
5. Therefore, you will no longer be allowed to own or carry anything more dangerous than a vegetable peeler. Although a permit will be required if you wish to carry a vegetable peeler in public.
6. All intersections will be replaced with roundabouts, and you will start driving on the left side with immediate effect. At the same time, you will go metric with immediate effect and without the benefit of conversion

tables. Both roundabouts and metrication will help you understand the British sense of humour.

7. The former USA will adopt UK prices on petrol (which you have been calling gasoline or 'gas') of roughly $10/US gallon. Get used to it.

8. You will learn to make real chips. Those things you call French fries are not real chips, and those things you insist on calling potato chips are properly called crisps. Real chips are thick cut, fried in animal fat, and dressed not with catsup but with vinegar.

9. The cold, tasteless stuff you insist on calling beer is not actually beer at all. Henceforth, only proper British Bitter will be referred to as beer, and European brews of known and accepted provenance will be referred to as Lager. South African beer is also acceptable, as they are pound for pound the greatest sporting nation on earth and it can only be due to the beer. They are also part of the British Commonwealth - see what it did for them. American brands will be referred to as Near-Frozen Gnat's Urine, so that all can be sold without risk of further confusion.

10. Hollywood will be required occasionally to cast English actors as good guys. Hollywood will also be required to cast English actors to play English characters. Watching Andie Macdowell attempt English dialect in Four Weddings and a Funeral was an experience akin to having one's ears removed with a cheese grater.

11. You will cease playing American football. There is only one kind of proper football; you call it soccer. Those of you brave enough will, in time, be allowed to play rugby (which has some similarities to American football, but does not involve stopping for a rest every twenty seconds or wearing full kevlar body armour like a bunch of nancies).

12. Further, you will stop playing baseball. It is not reasonable to host an event called the World Series for a game which is not played outside of America. Since only 2.1% of you are aware there is a world beyond

your borders, your error is understandable. You will learn cricket, and we will let you face the South Africans first to take the sting out of their deliveries.
13. You must tell us who killed JFK. It's been driving us mad.
14. An internal revenue agent (i.e. tax collector) from Her Majesty's Government will be with you shortly to ensure the acquisition of all monies due (backdated to 1776).
15. Daily Tea Time begins promptly at 4 pm with proper cups, with saucers, and never mugs, with high quality biscuits (cookies) and cakes; plus strawberries (with cream) when in season.

God Save the Queen!

CHAPTER 16

BAR JOKES

$200 bargain:

A man is having a drink in a hotel lounge. A really beautiful woman sits down next to him.

He says, 'Can I buy you a drink?'

She smiles and says 'Yes, thank you.'

For the next hour they chit chat and have a couple more drinks. Then, she turns to him, places her hand on his thigh, leans over to give him a better view down her plunging neck line. She looks him in the eyes and says, 'Sir, I will do anything you want of me for $200.00. I don't care what it is, $200.00 and it's yours, I will do it.'

The man is amazed, takes out his wallet and places $200.00 on the bar, leans close to her and says... 'Paint my house.'

Martial Arts:

I was standing at the bar of Terminal 3 International Airport when this small Chinese guy comes in, stands next to me and starts drinking a beer.

I asked him, 'Do you know any of those martial arts things, like Kung-Fu, Karate or Ju-Jitsu?'

He says 'No, why the fuck you ask me that? Is it because I'm Chinese?'

'No,' I said, 'It's because you're drinking my beer, you little prick.'

IQ levels:

A guy goes into a bar on Georgia Street, and is surprised to see a robot bartender. The robot asked, 'What will you have, sir?'

'Whiskey.' the guy replied.

The robot brought back his drink and asked, 'What's your IQ?'

'168,' he replied.

The robot begins to talk about physics, space exploration, and medical technology. When our guy left the bar, he got curious about the robot's responses, so he decided to go back.

The robot asked, 'What's your drink?'

Once again, our guy replied, 'Whiskey.'

The robot returned with his drink and asked, 'What's your IQ?'

The man replied, '100.'

The robot started a discussion about NasCar, Budweiser, the Lions and the Canucks. The man finished his drink, left, but becomes so interested in his 'experiment' that he decided to try something different.

He entered the bar and, as usual, the robot asked him what he wanted to drink.

The man replied, 'Whiskey.'

The robot brought the drink and asked, 'What's your IQ?'

The man answered, '50.'

The robot leaned in really close and asked,

'Did you watch the football game last night?'

Reindeer:

One evening in a busy lounge, a reindeer walked in the door, bellied up to the bar and ordered a beer. Without batting an eye, the bartender poured the drink, set it in front of the reindeer, and accepted the ten-dollar note from the reindeer's hoof. As he handed the reindeer some coins in change he said, 'You know, I think you're the first reindeer I've ever seen in here.'

The reindeer looked hard at the hoof-full of change and said, 'Hmmmpf. Let me tell you something, mate. At these prices, I'm the last reindeer you'll see in here.'

The Pirate:

One day a Pirate and a bartender were talking to each other in a bar. The bartender asked the pirate, 'Where did ya get that peg-leg from?'

The pirate responded, 'We were sailing the seas when a big ol' shark came up to me while I was swimmin' and bit off me leg.'

Later, the bartender asked, 'Where did you get that hook then?'

The pirate responded, 'Well, me crew and I were in a battle and I got cut through the bone.'

The bartender then asked, 'Then where did you get the eye patch from?'

The pirate said, 'In a harbour, I looked at a gull flying overhead and it pooped right in me eye.'

The bartender was puzzled and asked the pirate, 'How would that make you get an eye patch?'

The pirate responded, 'First day with the hook.'

Two Brothers:

An Irish man walks into a pub. The bartender asks him, 'What'll you have?'

The man replies, 'Give me three pints of Guinness please.'

So the bartender brings him three pints and the man proceeds to alternatively sip one, then the other, then the third until they're gone. He then orders three more.

The bartender says, 'Sir, I know you like them cold. You don't have to order three at a time. I can keep an eye on it and when you get low I'll bring you a fresh cold one.'

The man says, 'You don't understand, I have two brothers. One is in Australia and one in the States. We made a vow to each other that every Saturday night we'd still drink together. So right now, my brothers have three Guinnes Stouts too, and we're drinking together.'

The bartender thought that was a wonderful tradition. Every week the man came in and ordered three beers. Then one week he came in and ordered only two. He drank them and then ordered two more.

The bartender said to him, 'I know what your tradition is, and I'd just like to say that I'm sorry that one of your brothers died.'

The man replied, 'Oh, me brothers are fine... I just quit drinking.'

This 'N That:

- Paddy texts his wife, 'Mary, I'm just having one more pint with the lads. If I'm not back in twenty minutes, read this message again.'
- A drunk walks into a bar with jumper cables around his neck. The bartender says, 'You can stay, but don't try to start anything!'
- I drink wine because the doctor said I shouldn't keep things bottled up.
- The answer may not lie at the bottom of a bottle of wine, but you should at least check.
- It's funny how eight glasses of water a day seems impossible, but eight glasses of wine can be done in one meal.
- Every box of raisins is a tragic story of grapes that could have been wine.

- A fellow in a bar notices a woman, always alone, who comes in on a fairly regular basis.

  After the second week, he makes his move. 'No thank you,' she answers politely. 'This may sound rather odd in this day and age, but I'm keeping myself pure until I meet the man I love.'

  'That must be rather difficult,' the man replies.

  'Oh, I don't mind too much,' she says, 'but, it has my husband pretty upset.'

- A bloke was chatting up a pretty girl in the pub and telling her of his uncanny ability to be able to tell the day any woman was born just by holding her chest in his hands.
  The girl thought he was having her on but eventually curiosity got the better of her and said he could test out his 'gift.'

  He stood there for a few minutes holding her ample chest until she said, 'That's enough. When was I born.'

  He waited a moment and stepped back before he replied, 'Yesterday.'

- An old lady goes to the bar on a cruise ship and orders a Scotch with two drops of water. As the bartender gives her the drink she says, 'I'm on this cruise to celebrate my eightieth birthday and its today.'

  The bartender says, 'Well, since it's your birthday, I'll buy you a drink. In fact, this one is on me.'

  As the woman finishes her drink, the woman to her right says, 'I would like to buy you a drink, too.'

  The old woman says, 'Thank you. Bartender, I want a Scotch with two drops of water please.'

  'Coming up,' says the bartender.

As she finishes that drink, the man to her left says, 'I would like to buy you one also.'

The old woman says, 'Well thank you. Bartender, I want another Scotch with two drops of water.'

'Coming right up,' the bartender says.

As he gives her the drink, he says, 'Ma'am, I'm dying of curiosity. Why the Scotch with only two drops of water?'

The old woman replies, 'Sonny, when you're my age, you've learned how to hold your liquor, but holding your water however, is a whole other issue.'

- Two men, Jim and John, were walking their dogs when they passed by a restaurant/bar.

'Let's go in and get something to eat,' Jim suggested.

'We can't,' replied John. 'Don't you see the sign that says, *No Pets Allowed?*'

'Aah that sign,' said Jim. 'Don't worry about it.'

Taking out a pair of sunglasses, he walked up to the door. As he tried walking into the restaurant, he got stopped at the door. 'Sorry no pets allowed. Can't you see?' said the doorman.

Jim replied, 'I'm blind. This is my seeing-eye-dog.'

'But it's a Doberman Pincer. Who uses a Doberman Pincher as a seeing eye dog?'

'Oh,' Jim responded. 'You must have not heard, this is the latest type of seeing-eye-dog. They do a very good job.'

Seeing it worked for Jim, John tries walking in with his Chihuahua. Even before he could open his mouth, the doorman said, 'Don't tell me that a Chihuahua is the latest type of seeing-eye-dog?'

Thinking quickly, John responded in an angry voice, 'You mean they gave me a Chihuahua?!'

CHAPTER 17

HIGH TECHNOLOGY

I love my computer, because my friends live in it!

Rocket Science

Sometimes it DOES take a Rocket Scientist!! (true story)

Scientists at Rolls Royce built a gun specifically to launch dead chickens at the windshields of airliners and military jets all travelling at maximum velocity. The idea is to simulate the frequent incidents of collisions with airborne fowl to test the strength of the windshields.

American engineers heard about the gun and were eager to test it on the Windshields of their new high speed trains. Arrangements were made, and a gun was sent to the American engineers.

When the gun was fired, the engineers stood shocked as the chicken shot out of the barrel, crashed into the shatterproof shield, smashed it to smithereens, blasted through the control console, snapped the engineer's back-rest in two and embedded itself in the back wall of the cabin like an arrow shot from a bow.

The horrified Yanks sent Rolls Royce the disastrous results of the experiment, along with the designs of the windshield and begged the British scientists for suggestions.

You're going to love this...

Rolls Royce responded with a one-line memo: 'Defrost the chicken.'

The King and Queen go fishing:

Once upon a time there was a King who wanted to go fishing. He called the royal weather forecaster and inquired as to the weather forecast for the next few hours. The weatherman assured him that there was no chance of rain in the coming days.

So the King went fishing with his wife, the Queen.

On the way he met a farmer on his donkey. Upon seeing the King the farmer said, 'Your Majesty, you should return to the palace at once because in just a short time I expect a huge amount of rain to fall in this area.'

The King, polite and considerate, replied, 'I hold the palace meteorologist in high regard. He is an extensively educated and experienced professional. And besides, I pay him very high wages. He gave me a very different forecast. I trust him and I will continue on my way.'

So he continued on his way. However, a short time later a torrential rain fell from the sky. The King and Queen were totally soaked and their entourage chuckled upon seeing them in such a shameful condition.

Furious, the King returned to the palace and gave the order to fire the professional. Then he sent for the farmer and offered him the prestigious and high paying role of royal forecaster.

The farmer said, 'Your Majesty, I do not know anything about forecasting. I obtain my information from my donkey. If I see my donkey's ears drooping, it means with certainty that it will rain.'

So the King hired the donkey and thus began the practice of hiring dumb asses to work in the government and occupy its highest and most influential positions. And the practice is unbroken to this date...

Not all thieves are stupid:

Long-term parking:

Some people left their car in the long-term parking at San Jose while away, and someone broke into the car. Using the information on the car's registration in the glove compartment, they drove the car to the people's home in Pebble Beach and robbed it. So I guess if we are going to leave the car in long-term parking, we should NOT leave the registration/insurance cards in it, nor your remote garage door opener. This gives us something to think about with all our new electronic technology.

GPS:

Someone had their car broken into while they were at a football game. Their car was parked on the green which was adjacent to the football stadium and specially allotted to football fans. Things stolen from the car included a garage door remote control, some money and a GPS which had been prominently mounted on the dashboard. When the victims got home, they found that their house had been ransacked and just about everything worth anything had been stolen. The thieves had used the GPS to guide them to the house. They then used the garage remote control to open the garage door and gain entry to the house. The thieves knew the owners were at the football game, they knew what time the game was scheduled to finish and so they knew how much time they had to clean out the house.

It would appear that they had brought a truck to empty the house of its contents. Something to consider if you have a GPS - don't put your home address in it... Put a nearby address (like a store or gas station) so you can still find your way home if you need to, but no one else would know where you live if your GPS is stolen.

Cell phones:

I never thought of this. This lady has now changed her habit of how she lists her names on her cell phone after her handbag was stolen. Her handbag, which contained her cell phone, credit card, wallet, etc., was stolen. Twenty minutes later when she called her hubby, from a pay phone telling him what had happened, hubby says, 'I received your text asking about our Pin number and I replied a little while ago.'

When they rushed down to the bank, the bank staff told them all the money was already withdrawn. The thief had actually used the stolen cell phone to text 'hubby' in the contact list and got hold of the pin number. Within 20 minutes the theif had withdrawn all the money from their bank account.

Moral of the lesson:

a. Do not disclose the relationship between you and the people in your contact list. Avoid using names like Home, Honey, Hubby, Sweetheart, Dad, Mom, etc.
b. And very importantly, when sensitive info is being asked through texts, confirm by calling back.
c. Also, when you're being texted by friends or family to meet them somewhere, be sure to call back to confirm that the message came from them. If you don't reach them, be very careful about going places to meet 'family and friends' who text you.

Purse in the grocery cart scam:

A lady went grocery-shopping at a local mall and left her purse sitting in the children's seat of the cart while she reached something off a shelf. Her wallet was stolen, and she reported it to the store personnel. After returning home, she received a phone call from the Mall Security to say that they had her wallet and that although there was no money in it, it did still hold her personal papers. She immediately went to pick up her wallet, only to be told by Mall Security that they had not called her.

By the time she returned home again, her house had been broken into and burglarized. The thieves knew that by calling and saying they were from Mall Security, they could lure her out of her house long enough for them to burglarize it.

CHAPTER 18

RULES FOR LIVING

The meaning of life ...

- As we grow older, and hence wiser, we slowly realize that wearing a $300 or $30.00 watch - they both tell the same time.
- Whether we carry a $300 or $30.00 wallet/handbag, the amount of money inside is the same.
- Whether the house we live in is 30 or 300 sqm, the loneliness is the same.
- I've never met a strong person with an easy past. Get over your past – keep looking forward with optimism.
- Hopefully, one day you will realize, your true inner happiness does not come from the material things of this world.
- Whether you fly first, business or economy class, if the plane goes down, you go down with it.
- Worry doesn't take away tomorrow's troubles – it takes away today's peace.

Therefore, I hope you realize, when you have mates, buddies and old friends, brothers and sisters, who you chat with, laugh with, talk with, have sing songs with, talk about north-south-east-west or heaven and earth. That is true happiness!!

Rules for Living:

Take chances; tell the truth; learn to say 'NO;' spend money on things you love; laugh till your stomach hurts; dance even if you're bad at it; pose for stupid photos; be child-like.

Moral: Death is not the greatest loss in life – the greatest loss is when life dies inside you while you are still alive. Always make sure you have something to 'get up for.'

Five rules to remember in life:

1. Money cannot buy happiness - but it's far more comfortable to cry in a Porsche than on a bicycle.
2. Forgive your enemy - but remember the asshole's name.
3. If you help someone when they're in trouble - they will remember you when they're in trouble again.
4. Alcohol does not solve any problems - but then neither does milk.

And my personal favourite:

5. Many people are alive only because it's illegal to shoot them.

Bonus rule:

Condoms do not guarantee safe sex. A friend of mine was wearing one when he was shot by the woman's husband.

Undeniable Facts of Life:

1. Don't educate your children to be rich. Educate them to be happy so when they grow up they will know the value of things not the price.
2. Best awarded words in London: 'Eat your food as your medicines, otherwise you have to eat medicines as your food.'
3. The one who loves you will never leave you because even if there are 100 reasons to give up s/he will find one reason to hold on.
4. There is a big difference between a human being and being human. Only a few really understand it.
5. You are loved when you are born. You will be loved when you die. In between, you have to manage!
6. Never confuse education with intelligence.
7. Reading can seriously damage your ignorance.
8. How to stop time: kiss. How to travel in time: read. How to escape time: music.
9. Having a soulmate is not always about love. You can find your soulmate in a friendship too.

10. The ability to speak several languages is an asset, but the ability to keep your mouth shut in any language is priceless.
11. A scientist will read dozens of books in his lifetime but still believes he has a lot more to learn. Some religious people barely read one book and think they know it all.
12. If you just want to walk fast, walk alone, but if you want to walk far, walk together.

Six Best Doctors in the World:

1. Sunlight
2. Rest
3. Exercise
4. Diet
5. Self Confidence and
6. Friends

Maintain them in all stages of Life and enjoy healthy life.

Bob Hope

On his deathbed they asked him where he wanted to be buried. He replied, 'Surprise me!'

He lived to be 100 years of age. I always enjoyed him, his movies, and his show. He touched a lot of lives during his life. I thought you might enjoy a bit of memory touching. Enjoy and recall a neat comedian. This is a tribute to a man who DID make a difference

On turning 70: 'I still chase women, but only downhill.'

On turning 80: 'That's the time of life when your birthday suit needs pressing.'

On turning 90: 'You know you're getting old when the candles cost more than the cake.'

On turning 100: 'I don't feel old. In fact, I don't feel anything until noon. Then it's time for my nap.'

On giving up his career in boxing: 'I ruined my hands in the ring. The referee kept stepping on them.'

On never winning an Oscar: 'Welcome to the Academy Awards, or as it's called at my home 'Passover.'

On golf: 'Golf is my profession. Show business is just to pay the green fees.'

On Presidents: 'I have performed for 12 Presidents, but entertained only six.'

On why he chose show business for his career: 'When I was born, the doctor said to my mother, 'Congratulations, you have an eight-pound ham.'

On receiving the Congressional Gold Metal: 'I feel very humble, but I think I have the strength of character to fight it.'

On his family's early poverty: 'Four of us slept in one bed. When it got cold, Mother threw on another brother.'

On his six brothers: 'That's how I learned to dance – waiting for the bathroom.'

On his early failures: 'I would not have had anything to eat if it wasn't for the stuff the audience threw at me.'

On going to Heaven: 'I've done benefits for all religions. I'd hate to blow the hereafter on a technicality.'

Failed relationships:

All failed relationships hurt, but losing someone who doesn't appreciate and respect you is actually a gain, not a loss.

Christmas message from the boss:

Please be advised that all employees planning to dash through the snow in a one-horse open sleigh, going over the fields and laughing all the way are required to undergo a Risk Assessment addressing the safety of open sleighs.

The assessment must also consider whether it is appropriate to use only one horse for such a venture, particularly where there are multiple passengers.

Please note that permission must also be obtained in writing from landowners before their fields may be entered. To avoid offending those not participating in celebrations, we request that laughter is moderate only and not loud enough to be considered a noise nuisance.

Benches, stools and orthopaedic chairs are now available for collection by any shepherds planning or required to watch their flocks at night. While provision has also been made for remote monitoring of flocks by CCTV cameras from a centrally heated shepherd observation hut, all facility users are reminded that an emergency response plan must be submitted to account for known risks to the flocks. The angel of the Lord is additionally reminded that prior to shining his/her glory all around s/he must confirm that all shepherds are wearing appropriate Personal Protective Equipment to account for the harmful effects of UVA, UVB and the overwhelming effects of Glory.

Following last year's well-publicised case, everyone is advised that legislation prohibits any comment with regard to the redness of any part of Mr. R. Reindeer. Further to this, exclusion of Mr. R Reindeer from reindeer games will be considered discriminatory and disciplinary action will be taken against those found guilty of this offence.

While it is acknowledged that gift-bearing is commonly practiced in various parts of the world, particularly the Orient, everyone is reminded that the bearing of gifts is subject to Hospitality Guidelines and all gifts must be registered. This applies regardless of the individual, even royal personages. It is particularly noted that direct gifts of currency or gold are specifically precluded under provisions of the Foreign Corrupt Practices Act. Further, caution is advised regarding other common gifts, such as aromatic resins that may initiate allergic reactions.

Finally, for those involved in the recent case of the infant found tucked up in a manger without any crib for a bed, Social Services have been advised and will be arriving shortly.

Wishing you a very Merry Christmas - be safe out there.

A letter from the post office:

This is absolutely the best!! We don't know who replied, but there is a beautiful soul working in the dead letter office who understands love.

Our 14-year-old dog Abbey died last month. The day after she passed away my four-year-old daughter Meredith was crying and talking about how much she missed Abbey. She asked if we could write a letter to God so that when Abbey got to heaven, God would recognize her.

I told her that I thought that we could, so she dictated these words:

Dear God,

Will you please take care of my dog? Abbey died yesterday and is with you in heaven. I miss her very much.

I'm happy that you let me have her as my dog even though she got sick. I hope you will play with her. She likes to swim and play with balls.

I am sending a picture of her so when you see her you will know that she is my dog.

I really miss her.

Love, Meredith

We put the letter in an envelope with a picture of Abbey and Meredith, addressed it to God/Heaven. We put our return address on it. Meredith pasted several stamps on the front of the envelope because she said it would take lots of stamps to get the letter all the way to heaven. That afternoon she dropped it into the letter box at the post office.

A few days later, she asked if God had gotten the letter yet. I told her that I thought He had.

Yesterday, there was a package wrapped in gold paper on our front porch addressed, 'To Meredith' in an unfamiliar hand. Meredith opened it. Inside was a book by Mr. Rogers called, 'When a Pet Dies.' Taped to the inside front cover was the letter we had written to God in its opened envelope. On the opposite page was the picture of Abbey and Meredith and this note:

Dear Meredith,

Abbey arrived safely in heaven. Having the picture was a big help and I recognized her right away. Abbey isn't sick any more. Her spirit is here with me just like it stays in your heart.

Abbey loved being your dog. Since we don't need our bodies in heaven, I don't have any pockets to keep your picture in so I'm sending it back to you in this little book for you to keep and have something to remember Abbey by.

Thank you for the beautiful letter and thank your mother for helping you write it and sending it to me. What a wonderful mother you have. I picked her especially for you.

I send my blessings every day and remember that I love you very much.

By the way, I'm easy to find. I am wherever there is love.

Love,

God

Life's truths:

'You have not lived today until you have done something for someone who can never repay you.' - John Bunyan

'Good friends are like stars. You don't always see them, but you know they're always there.'

I'm an Optipessimist. My glass is half full, but I'm wondering who the hell drank the other half?

Ice Cream:

One day I had lunch with some old friends. Jim, a short, balding golfer type, about 85-years old, came along with them. All in all, it was a pleasant bunch. When the menus were presented, my friends and I ordered salads, sandwiches, and soups, except for Jim who said, 'A large piece of home-made apple pie, heated please along with two large scoops of vanilla ice cream.'

I wasn't sure my ears heard him right, and the others were aghast, when Jim continued, completely unabashed. We tried to act quite nonchalant, as if people did this all the time, but when our orders were brought out, I didn't enjoy eating mine.

I couldn't take my eyes off of Jim as I watched him savouring each bite of his pie a-la-mode. The other guys just grinned in disbelief as they silently ate their lunches.

The next time I went out to eat, I called Jim and invited him to join me. I lunched on a white meat tuna sandwich, while he ordered a chocolate parfait. Since I was chuckling, he wanted to know if he amused me.

I answered, 'Yes, you certainly do, but you also confuse me. How come you always order such rich desserts, while I feel like I must be sensible in my food choices?'

He laughed and said 'I'm tasting all that is possible for me to taste. I try to eat the food I need and do the things I should in order to stay healthy, but life's too short, my friend. I hate missing out on something good. This year I realized how old I was. (He grinned) I've never been this old before, so, while I'm still here, I've decided it's time to try all those things that, for years, I've been ignoring.'

He continued, 'I haven't smelled all the flowers yet. There are too many trout streams I haven't fished. There's more fudge sundaes to wolf down and kites to be flown overhead. There are too many golf courses I haven't played. I've not laughed at all the jokes. I've missed a lot of sporting events and potato chips and cokes.'

'I want to wade again in water and feel ocean spray on my face. I want to sit in a country church once more and thank God for His grace.'

'I want peanut butter every day spread on my morning toast. I want un-timed long distance calls to the ones I love the most.'

'I haven't cried at all the movies yet, or walked in the morning rain. I need to feel wind on my face. I want to be in love again.'

'So, if I choose to have dessert, instead of having dinner, then should I die before night fall, I'd say I died a winner, because I missed out on nothing. I filled my heart's desire. I had that final piece of pie before my life expired.'

With that, I called the waitress over. 'I've changed my mind,' I said. 'I want what he's having, only add some more whipped cream!'

Live well, love much, and laugh often. Be happy and enjoy doing whatever your heart desires. You only go around once on this crazy planet. Be mindful that happiness isn't based on possessions, power, or prestige, but on relationships with people we like, respect, and enjoy spending time with. Remember that while money talks, *ice cream sings!*

Potato Chips:

A little boy wanted to meet God. He knew it was a long trip to where God lived so he packed his suitcase with a bag of potato chips and a six-pack of root beer and started his journey.

When he had gone about three blocks, he met an old man who was sitting in the park, just staring at some pigeons. The boy sat down next to him and opened his suitcase. He was about to take a drink from his root beer when he noticed that the old man looked hungry, so he offered him some chips. He gratefully accepted them and smiled at him.

His smile was so special that the boy wanted to see it again, so he offered him a root beer. Again, the old man smiled at him. The boy was delighted! They sat there all afternoon eating and smiling, but they never said a word.

As twilight approached, the boy realized how tired he was and he got up to leave. But before he had gone more than a few steps, he turned around, ran back to the old man, and gave him a hug. He gave him his biggest smile ever.

When the boy opened the door to his own house a short time later, his mother was surprised by the look of joy on his face. She asked him, 'What did you do today that made you so happy?'

He replied, 'I had lunch with God.' Before his mother could respond, he added, 'You know what? He's got the most beautiful smile I've ever seen!'

Meanwhile, the old man, also radiant with joy, returned to his home. His son was stunned by the look of peace on his face and he asked, 'Dad, what did you do today that made you so happy?'

He replied 'I ate potato chips in the park with God.' Before his son could respond, he added, 'You know, he's much younger than I expected.'

Too often we underestimate the power of a smile, a kind word, a listening ear, an honest compliment, or the smallest act of caring, all of which have the potential to turn a life around. People come into our lives for a reason, a season, or a lifetime! Embrace all equally! Have lunch with God. Bring chips and root beer.

CHAPTER 19

ON THE SERIOUS SIDE

Life Lesson:

At the prodding of my friends, I am writing this story. My name is Mildred Honor. I am a former elementary school Music Teacher from Des Moines, Iowa. I have always supplemented my income by teaching piano lessons, something I have done for over 30 years. During those years, I found that children have many levels of musical ability, and even though I have never had a prodigy, I have taught some very talented students. However, I have also had my share of what I call 'Musically challenged pupils.'

One such pupil being Robby who was eleven years old when his mother (a single mom) dropped him off for his first piano lesson.

I prefer that Students (especially boys) begin at an earlier age, which I explained to Robby, but Robby said that it had always been his mother's dream to hear him play the piano, so I took him as a student.

At the end of each weekly lesson he would always say 'My Mom's going to hear me play someday.' But to me, it seemed hopeless, he just did not have any in-born ability. I only knew his mother from a distance as she dropped Robby off or waited in her aged car to pick him up. She always waved and smiled, but never dropped in.

Then one day Robby stopped coming for his Lessons. I thought about calling him, but assumed that because of his lack of ability he had decided to pursue something else. I was also glad that he had stopped coming. He was a bad advertisement for my teaching!

Several weeks later I mailed a flyer recital to the students' homes. To my surprise, Robby (who had received a flyer) asked if he could be in the recital. I told him that the recital was for current pupils and that because he had dropped out, he really did not qualify.

He told me that his mother had been sick and unable to take him to his piano lessons, but that he had been practicing. 'Please Miss Honor, I've just got to play,' he insisted.

I don't know what led me to allow him to play in the recital - perhaps it was his insistence or maybe something inside of me saying that it would be all right.

The night of the recital came and the high school gymnasium was packed with parents, relatives and friends. I put Robby last in the program, just before I was to come up and thank all the students and play a finishing piece. I thought that any damage he might do would come at the end of the program and I could always salvage his poor performance through my 'curtain closer.'

Well, the recital went off without a hitch, the students had been practicing and it showed. When Robby came up on the stage, his clothes were wrinkled and his hair looked as though he had run an egg beater through it.

'Why wasn't he dressed up like the other students?' I thought. 'Why didn't his mother at least make him comb his hair for this special night?'

Robby pulled out the piano bench, and I was surprised when he announced that he had chosen to play Mozart's Concerto No.21 in C Major. I was not prepared for what I heard next. His fingers were light on the keys, they even danced nimbly on the ivories. He went from pianissimo to fortissimo, from allegro to virtuoso; his suspended cords that Mozart demands were magnificent! Never had I heard Mozart played so well by anyone his age.

After six and a half minutes, he ended in a grand crescendo, and everyone was on their feet in wild applause!!! Overcome and in tears, I ran up on stage and put my arms around Robby.

'I have never heard you play like that Robby, how did you do it?'

Through the microphone Robby explained: 'Well, Miss Honor, remember I told you that my Mom was sick? Well, she actually had cancer and passed away this morning. And well... she was born deaf, so tonight was the first time she had ever heard me play, and I wanted to make it special.'

There wasn't a dry eye in the house that evening. As people from social services led Robby from the stage to be placed in to foster care, I noticed that even their eyes were red and puffy. I thought to myself then how much richer my life had been for taking Robby as my pupil.

So, I have never had a prodigy, but that night I became a prodigy of Robby. He was the teacher and I was the pupil, for he had taught me the meaning of perseverance and love and believing in yourself, and maybe even taking a chance on someone and you didn't know why.

Many years later, Robby was killed in the senseless bombing of the Alfred P. Murray Federal Building in Oklahoma City in April, 1995.

Life's trials and tribulations:

One day, a man walking down a path saw a butterfly cocoon that was about to open. As he watched, a small opening appeared in the cocoon; the man sat and watched the butterfly for several hours as it struggled to force its body through that little hole. 'Then it seemed to stop making any progress. It appeared it had gotten as far as it could and it could go no further.'

So the man decided to help the butterfly. He took a pair of tiny scissors and opened the cocoon. The butterfly then emerged easily. But it had a withered body. It was tiny and its wings were shrivelled.

The man continued to watch because he expected the wings would open and expand and be able to support the butterfly's body.

What the man, in his kindness and his goodwill, did not understand, was that the restricting cocoon and the struggle required for the butterfly to get through the tiny opening were nature's way of forcing fluid from the body of the butterfly into its wings so that it would be ready for flight once it achieved its freedom from the cocoon.

Sometimes struggles are exactly what we need in our lives. If we were allowed to go through our life without any obstacles, it would cripple us. We would not be as strong as we could have been and would never be able to fly.

- We asked for strength and we're given difficulties to make us strong.
- We ask for wisdom and we're given problems to solve.
- We ask for prosperity and are given a brain and brawn to work.
- We ask for courage and we're given obstacles to overcome.
- We ask for love and we're given troubled people to help.
- We ask for favours and we're given opportunities.
- We receive nothing we wanted, but received everything we needed.

Live life without fear. Confront all obstacles and know that you can overcome them. All you need to do is make the effort.

This is what Christmas is all about...

'Pa never had much compassion for the lazy or those who squandered their means and then never had enough for the necessities. But for those who were genuinely in need, his heart was as big as all outdoors. It was from him that I learned the greatest joy in life comes from giving, not from receiving.

It was Christmas Eve 1881. I was fifteen years old and feeling like the world had caved in on me because there just hadn't been enough money to buy me the rifle that I'd wanted for Christmas. We did the chores early that night for some reason. I just figured Pa wanted a little extra time so we could read the Bible.

After supper was over I took my boots off and stretched out in front of the fireplace and waited for Pa to get down the old Bible. I was still feeling sorry for myself and, to be honest, I wasn't in much of a mood to read Scriptures. But Pa didn't get the Bible, instead he bundled up again and went outside. I couldn't figure it out because we had already done all the chores. I didn't worry about it long though, I was too busy wallowing in self-pity.

Soon Pa came back in. It was a cold clear night out and there was ice in his beard. 'Come on, Matt,' he said. 'Bundle up good, it's cold out tonight.'

I was really upset then. Not only wasn't I getting the rifle for Christmas, now Pa was dragging me out in the cold, and for no earthly reason that I could see. We'd already done all the chores, and I couldn't think of anything else that needed doing, especially not on a night like this. But I knew Pa was not very patient at one dragging one's feet when he'd told them to do something, so I got up and put my boots back on and got my cap, coat, and mittens. Ma gave me a mysterious smile as I opened the door to leave the house. Something was up, but I didn't know what.

Outside, I became even more dismayed. There in front of the house was the work team, already hitched to the big sled. Whatever it was we were going to do wasn't going to be a short, quick, little job I could tell. We never hitched up this sled unless we were going to haul a big load. Pa was already up on the seat, reins in hand. I reluctantly climbed up beside him. The cold was already biting at me. I wasn't happy.

When I was on, Pa pulled the sled around the house and stopped in front of the woodshed. He got off and I followed. 'I think we'll put on the high sideboards,' he said. 'Here, help me.'

The high sideboards! It had been a bigger job than I wanted to do with just the low sideboards on, but whatever it was we were going to do would be a lot bigger with the high side boards on. After we had exchanged the sideboards, Pa went into the woodshed and came out with an armload of wood - the wood I'd spent all summer hauling down from the mountain, and then all fall sawing into blocks and splitting. What was he doing?

Finally, I said something. 'Pa,' I asked, 'what are you doing?'

'You been by the Widow Jensen's lately?' he asked. The Widow Jensen lived about two miles down the road. Her husband had died a year or so before and left her with three children, the oldest being eight. Sure, I'd been by, but so what?

'Yeah,' I said, 'Why?'

'I rode by just today,' Pa said. 'Little Jakey was out digging around in the woodpile trying to find a few chips. They're out of wood, Matt.'

That was all he said and then he turned and went back into the woodshed for another armload of wood. I followed him. We loaded the sled so high that I began to wonder if the horses would be able to pull it. Finally, Pa called a halt to our loading, then we went to the smoke house and Pa took down a big ham and a side of bacon. He handed them to me and told me to put them in the sled and wait.

When he returned he was carrying a sack of flour over his right shoulder and a smaller sack of something in his left hand. 'What's in the little sack?' I asked

'Shoes, they're out of shoes. Little Jakey just had gunny sacks wrapped around his feet when he was out in the woodpile this morning. I got the children a little candy too. It just wouldn't be Christmas without a little candy.'

We rode the two miles to Widow Jensen's pretty much in silence. I tried to think through what Pa was doing. We didn't have much by worldly standards. Of course, we did have a big woodpile, though most of what was left now was still in the form of logs that I would have to saw into blocks and split before we could use it. We also had meat and flour, so we could spare that, but I knew we didn't have any money, so why was Pa buying them shoes and candy? Really, why was he doing any of this? Widow Jensen had closer neighbours than us; it shouldn't have been our concern.

We came in from the blind side of the Jensen house and unloaded the wood as quietly as possible, then we took the meat and flour and shoes to the door. We knocked. The door opened a crack and a timid voice said, 'Who is it?'

'Lucas Miles, Ma'am, and my son, Matt, could we come in for a bit?'

Widow Jensen opened the door and let us in. She had a blanket wrapped around her shoulders. The children were wrapped in another and were sitting in front of the fireplace by a very small fire that hardly gave off any heat at all. Widow Jensen fumbled with a match and finally lit the lamp.

'We brought you a few things, Ma'am,' Pa said and set down the sack of flour. I put the meat on the table. Then Pa handed her the sack that had the shoes in it. She opened it hesitantly and took the shoes out one pair at a time. There was a pair for her and one for each of the children - sturdy shoes, the best, shoes that would last. I watched her carefully. She bit her lower lip to keep it from trembling and then tears filled her eyes and started running down her cheeks. She looked up at Pa like she wanted to say something, but it wouldn't come out.

'We brought a load of wood too, Ma'am,' Pa said. He turned to me and said, 'Matt, go bring in enough to last awhile. Let's get that fire up to size and heat this place up.'

I wasn't the same person when I went back out to bring in the wood. I had a big lump in my throat and as much as I hate to admit it, there were tears in my eyes too. In my mind I kept seeing those three kids huddled around the fireplace and their mother standing there with tears running down her cheeks with so much gratitude in her heart that she couldn't speak. My heart swelled within me and a joy that I'd never known before, filled my soul. I had given at Christmas many times before, but never when it had made so much difference. I could see we were literally saving the lives of these people.

I soon had the fire blazing and everyone's spirits soared. The kids started giggling when Pa handed them each a piece of candy and Widow Jensen looked on with a smile that probably hadn't crossed her face for a long time. She finally turned to us. 'God bless you,' she said. 'I know the Lord has sent you. The children and I have been praying that he would send one of his angels to spare us.'

In spite of myself, the lump returned to my throat and the tears welled up in my eyes again. I'd never thought of Pa in those exact terms before, but after Widow Jensen mentioned it I could see that it was probably true. I was sure that a better man than Pa had never walked the earth. I started remembering all the times he had gone out of his way for Ma and me, and many others. The list seemed endless as I thought on it. Pa insisted that everyone try on the shoes before we left. I was amazed when they all fit and I wondered how he had known what sizes to get. Then I guessed that if he was on an errand for the Lord that the Lord would make sure he got the right sizes.

Tears were running down Widow Jensen's face again when we stood up to leave. Pa took each of the kids in his big arms and gave them a hug. They clung to him and didn't want us to go. I could see that they missed their Pa, and I was glad that I still had mine. At the door Pa turned to Widow Jensen and said, 'The Mrs. wanted me to invite you and the children over for Christmas dinner tomorrow. The turkey will be more than the three of us can eat, and a man can get cantankerous if he has to eat turkey for too many meals. We'll be by to get you about eleven. It'll be nice to have some little ones around again. Matt, here, hasn't been little for quite a spell.'

I was the youngest. My two brothers and two sisters had all married and had moved away. Widow Jensen nodded and said, 'Thank you, Brother Miles. I don't have to say, 'May the Lord bless you, I know for certain that He will.'

Out on the sled I felt a warmth that came from deep within and I didn't even notice the cold. When we had gone a ways, Pa turned to me and said, 'Matt, I want you to know something. Your ma and me have been tucking a little money away here and there all year so we could buy that rifle for you, but we didn't have quite enough. Then yesterday a man who owed me a little money from years back came by to make things square. Your ma and me were real excited, thinking that now we could get you that rifle, and I started into town this morning to do just that, but on the way I saw little Jakey out scratching in the woodpile with his feet wrapped in those gunny sacks and I knew what I had to do. Son, I spent the money for shoes and a little candy for those children. I hope you understand.'

I understood, and my eyes became wet with tears again. I understood very well, and I was so glad Pa had done it. Now the rifle seemed very low on my list of priorities. Pa had given me a lot more. He had given me the look on Widow Jensen's face and the radiant smiles of her three children. For the rest of my life, whenever I saw any of the Jensen's, or split a block of wood, I remembered, and remembering brought back that same joy I felt riding home beside Pa that night. Pa had given me much more than a rifle that night, he had given me the best Christmas of my life.'

CONCLUSION

I hope you have enjoyed these jokes and thoughts enough to obtain Volumes 1, 2, 3, and 4 that cover humour and serious thoughts in different areas, so there's no repetition.

Laughter is an essential ingredient to everyday living. If you haven't had a laugh today - you're depriving yourself of enjoyment in life. Bring the jokes out when you're having a bad day - that's what I do. You'll find that things just get better.

If you wish to read books on more serious topics, please see the following information about how to order my other books and e-Books.

<u>www.dealingwithdifficultpeople.info</u>

www.ingramcontent.com/pod-product-compliance
Lightning Source LLC
LaVergne TN
LVHW051553070426
835507LV00021B/2555